MW01297844

COME ON IN

to Papa's Presence

by Christopher J. Olson

ISBN-13: 978-1986486101

ISBN-10: 1986486109

—

3

DEDICATION

I want to dedicate this book to:

- God the Father, God the Son, and God the Holy Spirit
- My wonderful parents, Jim and Faye Olson, who raised me in the things of God
- My amazing wife, Beth, who is my best friend, my life partner, and the best wife I could ever ask for
- My four wonderful children, Judah, Levi, Elijah, and Zoe, who I love so much
- My spiritual fathers, Bob Phillips who went to be with the Lord in 2017, and Leif Hetland, both to whom I owe a debt of gratitude

Table of Contents:

WARNING

While I believe the contents of this book will be a great blessing to any who would read it, at the same time we must recognize that only the Bible is God's infallible Word, not any other book by any man. If you're not consistently spending time in the Word of God, please put this book down and get into His Word first. If you feel that what I state in this book in anyway contradicts the Word of God, please by all means go with what is written in His Word and only prayerfully consider the contents of this book in light of God's Holy Word.

INTRODUCTION

I understand that the presence of God is a bit mystical. Different people have different ideas of what the Presence of God means. For the most part, unless otherwise specified, when I refer to the presence of God in this book, I am actually referring to the manifest presence of God: something that you can experience with your senses. I am not referring to the omnipresence of God, but to His tangible presence.

Therefore, when giving descriptions or principles of how to enter or access His presence, I am speaking of sensing His presence upon us and within us.
With all that being said, it is still ultimately all by faith. I want to explain what I mean by "it's by faith." First of all, let me explain what I don't mean.

I feel like much of the time in many parts of the church, when we speak of doing something by faith, we don't really expect an intended result. It's just kind of a vague concept that conveys the idea that God is way far away and somehow this idea of doing something by faith is almost a pretending with no real expectation of seeing any result manifested.

That is NOT what I mean. What I do mean however is that doing something in faith means that I am not ruled merely by my feelings, but I am ruled by truth, the truth of God's Word, the truth of who God is, who I am in Christ, and what He accomplished for us at the cross. That what He has made available to us today by His atoning sacrifice, is available to us regardless of our fluctuating and fleeting feelings. It's by faith.

I believe that if people apprehend the principles of this book by faith and learn to engage God's presence with the Word of God, they will begin to experience encounters in His manifest presence. His Word and His Spirit are not at odds with one another, for it is the Spirit Himself who wrote the Book.

Chapter 1
HOLY PRESENCE

As I stood there in the presence of God before these precious believers in an Asian country, the Spirit of God began to fill the room. Our purpose in ministering at this conference was to impact the lives of believers from a closed nation who suffer great persecution.

In that moment of joy filled ministry time, the environment began to change. As I could feel the holy presence of God beginning to fill the room. I stopped dead in my tracks and just stood there in silence waiting on God, to discern what the Father was doing.

As I quieted my heart and waited on the Lord, I suddenly began to hear a thump in the back of the room. A moment later, I hear a thud in another part of the room. I didn't know what was going on, other than I knew that God's presence was invading the room. It was a very sober time, it was a holy moment.

After another moment, I heard another thud and another thump from different areas in the room. It was then that I realized people were falling out in the Spirit without anyone laying hands on them, other than the sovereign hand of God, Himself.

These were not people who were accustomed to such experiences. Such manifestations were new to them. These were not planned nor contrived. It was simply the manifest presence of a holy, loving Father falling upon His children in an undeniable and overwhelming way.

In that place of His holy presence, God began to speak to us prophetically. At the same time, others began to hear the voices of the martyrs singing in heaven. It was quite overwhelming to even be in a meeting such as this, let alone to be the human instrument leading the meeting. It was quite humbling.

Until not that many years ago, such manifestations of God's presence in meetings I would lead were quite rare. There was a time not that long ago when I was quite skeptical of supposed "manifestations" of God's presence. I certainly didn't experience such things, and if somebody else said that they experienced it, well, let's just say I had my doubts.

All of this began to change a few years ago through a series of encounters that I had with the Lord and through Him teaching me in His Word. I want to invite you on this journey with me as we explore through encounters with the Holy Spirit: the Father's love, the beauty of Jesus, and the power of His written Word.

As we start this journey together, let's first take a look at principles from His Word which give us understanding as to how we access to the Father's presence. Before we go any further, I would like to pray for you.

Father, I come before You now, in the name of your dear Son Jesus Christ, and I thank you for this dearly loved one who is reading this book. They are so precious and valuable to You.

I bless them, and I thank You, Jesus, that You shed Your blood at the cross, and the veil was torn in two so that they could come boldly into Your presence and live there permanently as a beloved son or daughter.

Holy Spirit, I ask You to rest upon them, reveal more of Jesus to them, and speak to their spirit as they read this book. I bless them on their journey of going to a deeper, more intimate place in Papa's heart and presence. In Jesus' Name, Amen.

Chapter 2

LEGAL ACCESS

When we contemplate the idea of entering God's presence we have to recognize that it's a pretty daring and audacious thought. We aren't talking about entering the presence of just anyone, we are talking about the presence of God almighty, the most holy, all-powerful King of the Universe. He was, quite frankly, known to kill people in the Old Testament.

When we really consider whose presence we are talking about it is not only daunting, but could be considered downright scary.

A prerequisite for even approaching this subject is an attitude of humility and reverence. We are not going to explore the full meaning of the fear of the Lord in this book, nonetheless living a lifestyle in God's presence requires a very healthy dose of the fear of the Lord. *The friendship of the Lord is for those who fear Him.* Psalm 25:14 ESV

While I won't take time to give a full biblical definition to the fear of the Lord, let us at least understand that the true fear of the Lord causes us to run to God, not from Him.

The question is: what gives us the right to enter into

the presence of the holy, sovereign King of the universe even for a second?

If the answer to this is merely because God is love, then we have an incomplete answer. Why? Because God is and always has been pure, perfect love. He has always had perfect love toward every member of humanity since the beginning of human history, but that does not mean that mankind has always been able to enter His presence.

While God is pure perfect love, He is also perfectly holy and just. Therefore, as a loving Father, He always wanted us to live in His presence. At the same time, as a God of perfect holiness and justice, He could not allow guilty sinners to just enter His presence casually.

The barrier to His presence was never about a lack of love in the Father's heart, He has always been passionate about us. The problem has been on our end: our sin problem.

There was an incongruence between our nature; God is holy, and we were by birth unholy. God is righteous, and we were by nature unrighteous.

The "bad news" is this righteous, holy God can only have fellowship with and extend His manifest presence to people who are holy and righteous.

That leaves us with quite a dilemma. Thankfully God had a solution to our dilemma, and that is good news. That is what the gospel literally means: good news.

What Jesus did for us at the cross makes all the difference. The dilemma for most of us, I'm referring to those who have truly been born again by the Holy Spirit, is that we have longed for intimate fellowship with the Father. We have yearned to experience the reality of His presence but have felt like we don't qualify because God is holy, and we are not. He is righteous, and we are not.

This is exactly where the good news of the gospel comes in. You might say, "I've been a Christian for years. I still have this unfulfilled longing for His presence. I know the gospel, but it hasn't changed my inability to experience His presence."

That might be true if your only or main concept of the gospel is that our sins are forgiven and one day we will go to heaven. There is so much more to the gospel than our post death arrival through the pearly gates.

If you do not see that what Jesus accomplished at the cross changes your qualification to experience His presence, you will probably never or rarely experience His presence. In other words, what Jesus did at the cross has become our qualification to enter His presence. His atoning sacrifice *is* our qualification to enter His presence.

What took place at the cross was not just that He took our sin, but that He took on our unrighteous identity. Not only did He take our *unrighteous* identity at the cross, but He in exchange gave us His own *righteous* identity.

"For He made Him who knew no sin, to be sin for us, that we might become the righteousness of God in Him." 2 Corinthians 5:21 NKJV

When you realize that the only people that can have intimate fellowship with God are those who are holy and righteous, and that saddens you because you feel like you are not qualified, that just shows that you don't understand the fullness of what Jesus accomplished for us at the cross.

Many of us think of the gospel as only a change, not an exchange. Much of our perception of the gospel is that we give Jesus our sin, guilt, and shame, our bad stuff.

You might say, "Well, is that not true?" Yes, it is true, but it is only half the truth. If we live we only *half* of the truth, we can wind up with a *whole* lot of problems.

Yes, it is true that we give Him our bad stuff, but if we fail to see what He gives us in return, we have an insufficient view of the gospel. The gospel is not merely a change, but an exchange.

In an exchange, you give something to someone, and you get something in return. We give Him our sin; He gives us forgiveness. We give Him our unrighteousness; He gives us His righteousness. Paul makes this very clear in the verse we just looked at (2 Corinthians 5:21).

Other verses that speak of this exchange (that we not only give to Him, but we receive from Him in exchange) are:

"But He was pierced through for our transgressions, He was crushed for our iniquities; The chastening for our well-being fell upon Him, and by His scourging we are healed." Isaiah 53:5 NASB

"For you know the grace of our Lord Jesus Christ, that though He was rich, yet for your sake He became poor, so that you through His poverty might become rich." 2 Corinthians 8:9 NASB

"Christ redeemed us from the curse of the Law, having become a curse for us—for it is written, "CURSED IS EVERYONE WHO HANGS ON A TREE"—in order that in Christ Jesus the blessing of Abraham

might come to the Gentiles, so that we would receive the promise of the Spirit through faith." Galatians 3:13-14 NASB

We give Him our filthy garments. We are then to receive His robe of righteousness.

If your understanding of the gospel only includes the first half, praise God that you no longer have your garment of guilt and shame from your sin, but if you haven't received His robe in exchange, you're just left naked.

Naked. Actually, that is a pretty good description of how a lot of Christians still feel. Naked: awkward, uncomfortable, vulnerable.

Thank God that He takes away our filthy robe of unrighteousness. Hallelujah, but there is more to the gospel than this. He then clothes us with a new robe of righteousness, His very own righteousness!

Though it sounds almost too good to be true (that is the idea of the gospel) that we receive the same righteousness that Jesus Himself has, this is the beauty and glorious joy of the divine exchange in the gospel of Jesus Christ. He bore our rejection, so we could receive His acceptance.

Many times, when I go places to speak, I ask the people, "Who is more righteous, you or Jesus?"

About 99% of the time most people respond, "Jesus."

It might sound crazy to us, but if we've been made righteous by Jesus' own righteousness, if truly His righteousness is now our righteousness, we really can't say that we're less righteous than Jesus.

To believe anything less is to water down, minimize, and undervalue the glorious exchange of the gospel.

Think of it this way. Imagine Bill Gates loaned you a billion dollars, and you foolishly squandered it all and were left penniless with a billion-dollar debt and absolute inability to repay him. It would be glorious for him to say, "I forgive all your debt." You would shout for joy and weep tears of gratitude. You would be forever grateful, but at the end of the day, you would still be penniless.

That is how I viewed the gospel for many years. I was thankful my debt was cancelled, but still felt like I had nothing in my account. As glorious as it is that Jesus cancelled our debt at the cross, forgiving us all our sin, there is more to the gospel than that.

In the divine exchange, our bank account of righteousness (our debt) is not merely erased so that we're brought back to zero thus still being poverty stricken, rather God takes the perfect righteousness that is in Christ's account and transfers it all into our account.

It's like Bill Gates not only cancelling your debt but making you a joint signer on his bank account. Then if you were to ask the question, "Who is wealthier, you or Bill Gates?" the answer would be that you both have the same amount of wealth because you now share the same account. This is exactly what Jesus did for us. As joint heirs, we now share the same account. Romans 8:17

Jesus did not merely cancel our debt of sin, He came to restore us to the Father by making us perfectly righteous and giving us perfect acceptance with the Father.

If you still have an identity in which you see yourself as naked and poor before a holy God and don't understand the robe of Christ's righteousness that has been placed upon us, you will continue to see yourself as disqualified from entering God's presence and all of His blessings.

This is so important because the Father's arms are always open wide to his children with no condemnation, but if we don't believe it, we won't live in the good of it. As Jesus said in Matthew 9:29, *"As your faith is, so be it unto you."*

If you are not convinced that you are worthy to live in His presence, you won't. The more convinced you are of your righteous standing with the Father, that you've now been made acceptable to Him, the easier it will become to access His presence.

My hope is that as you continue to read more chapters throughout this book, you will not only be convinced that Jesus made you worthy to enter His presence, but that it is our privilege as new covenant sons and daughters to consistently live in the Father's presence as a lifestyle.

Chapter 3

THE BETTER COVENANT

Hebrews 8:6 says that we have a better covenant than the Old Covenant. It's easy to state in theological terms, but it's a whole other thing to wrap our hearts and brains around the shocking reality that what we have today is even better than what they had under the Old Covenant.

The entire Old Testament is one great summation of man's inability to keep covenant. Over and over again we have proved this inability by constantly breaking covenant with God as clearly displayed in the lives of the Israelites.

Mere human flesh cannot keep covenant with God, so God decided to become man in the flesh of Jesus Christ and has made covenant with Christ. Therefore, the challenge of the New Covenant was this: after mankind's inability to keep covenant was repeatedly exposed in the Old Testament, God still wanted to have covenant with us.

But the problem still remained that we could not keep covenant. God's solution was to become one of us in Jesus and make covenant with Christ, therefore making it possible for us to have covenant relationship with God through Christ.

If we're not in Christ, we're not in covenant relationship with God. But if we're in Christ, God has made covenant with us because we are in His Son.

Here's the deal: if we try to have a New Covenant relationship with God through an Old Covenant mindset, we will end in frustration and despair. At best we will occasionally touch the outer courts but never dwell in His manifest presence.

The Old Testament is wonderful, glorious, and powerful and has many great things for us to learn from it.

Paul says in 1 Corinthians 10:11 (regarding the story of the Old Testament) "*These things happened to them as examples and were written down as warnings for us.*"

I am *not* someone who would say that now that we have the New Testament we don't need the Old Testament. The law and the prophets foreshadowed and pointed to Christ. Christ in the New Covenant is the fulfillment of the law and the prophets.

Everything in the Old Covenant was pointing to the day when Messiah would come and establish us in a New Covenant relationship with God as Father. Now that this is come, we don't ignore the Old

Testament (we learn from it) but neither do we live under the Old Covenant.

We need to look at the law and the prophets through the lens of New Covenant grace.

There are some key differences between the Old Covenant and New Covenant.

The Old Covenant/law reveals sin.

The power of sin is the law. 1 Corinthians 15:56

Through the law we become conscience of sin. Romans 3:20

The New Covenant/grace reveals a new righteousness.

We become the righteousness of God. 2 Corinthians 5:21

But also, for us to whom God will credit righteousness. Romans 4:24

The law releases death.

For the letter kills. 2 Corinthians 3:6

The ministry that was engraved in letters on stone brought death. 2 Corinthians 3:7

It's a ministry that condemns men. 2 Corinthians 3:9

The Spirit releases life.

But the Spirit gives life. 2 Corinthians 3:6

The ministry of the Spirit brings righteousness. 2 Corinthians 3:9

Paul says in Galatians 3:21, *"For if a law had been given that could impart life, then righteousness would certainly have come by the law."*

The clear implication that Paul is communicating here is this: the law, in spite of how wonderful it is, is *not* capable of imparting life. As a wonderful standard, the law reveals mankind's emptiness and inability to live up to such a high moral standard and exposes our need for a Savior.

Then he goes on to say in Galatians 3:24, *So the law was put in charge to lead us to Christ that we might be justified by faith.*

To sum up what we've just been saying, the law exposes sin and condemns us. It cannot make us righteous. It cannot give us life. The best that it can do is point us to Christ who does impart life and who becomes our righteousness.

We actually become righteous with His righteousness. This is what Paul was telling us in 2 Corinthians 5:21, *God made Him who had no sin to be sin for us, **so that** in Him we might become the righteousness of God.*

Under the Old Covenant God's law could not make

us holy. It could only reveal to us that we ourselves were not holy. The best that it could do was to point us to the holy One.

Under the Old Covenant the law could not change us. It could not impart life nor make us righteous. It was ultimately a ministry that condemned. 2 Corinthians 3:8

There is a lot that we could say about the contrast between the Old and New Covenant and how much better the New Covenant is. But the main point we need to see in all of this is that what we have today through Christ is a better, complete, everlasting, and more glorious Covenant.

We cannot successfully function in the Kingdom today under the New Covenant while still trying to operate with an Old Covenant mentality. As a New Covenant believer, I must realize these spiritual realities today in my life:

- God is not just out there somewhere or up there in heaven far away. He dwells with me and in me, inside of me right now.

- While God is a good Father who will discipline me at times, He's not waiting to pour out His wrath on me. It was already poured out on Christ at the cross. I am no longer His enemy; I'm now His beloved adopted son.

- The demands of the law and the prophets were fulfilled in Christ.

- I no longer try to obey to become righteous. I've been declared righteous in Christ. Therefore, my obedience flows out of my new righteous nature/identity.

- I don't perform to be accepted. My actions flow out of His acceptance of me.

- He's more fully revealed as Father.

What does all this have to do with you and me living in His presence today? Everything! Jesus said in John 4:21b *You will worship the Father neither on this mountain nor in Jerusalem.*

Prior to this statement *the* place to worship was Jerusalem, but now we're in a new season of the New Covenant. It's a better Covenant where we can worship God in spirit and truth from Nepal, India, Brazil, Pakistan, Canada, and even Iowa. That's good news!

God has always been omnipresent, but He hasn't always been indwelling the life of the believer. Now, because we are the temple of the Holy Spirit (1 Corinthians 6:19), anywhere we go, He goes. We are no longer restricted by geography.

I know many people who have toured Israel and were very blessed. As of the writing of this book, I haven't had the privilege of doing so. Aren't you so glad that you don't have to travel all the way to Jerusalem to worship and to experience your Father's presence?

When Jesus died on the cross, the veil that separated us from His holy presence was torn in two from top to bottom. (Luke 23:45) That veil has been forever removed for the believer. Now, in Christ we have continuous access to the Father's holy presence.

Stop living with an Old Covenant mindset and dive into the blessings of New Covenant reality in Christ Jesus. The law and the prophets were fulfilled, the veil was torn, and His precious blood cleanses you perfectly. So, don't shrink back in the shadows of shame, but come on into Papa's presence.

Chapter 4

BY FAITH

In this chapter as we look at the concept of living in God's presence by faith, I want to start off by addressing what I don't mean. When you hear the words "by faith" what comes to your mind? Does pretend? Not Real? Make believe or simply by faith means we will never feel anything until we get to heaven. Meanwhile while we're on Earth we will experience nothing until we get to heaven. Are those some of the concepts that come to your mind when you hear "by faith"?

That is *not* what I mean.

To give you an example of what I am talking about, Paul speaks in Romans 6 how we as believers died with Christ. Then he goes on to say, therefore reckon yourself dead to sin. In other words, what he is saying is, this right here is spiritual reality (we died with Christ). Therefore, begin to look at your life through the lens of this new spiritual reality and consider and declare it to be so.

Paul is saying this is truth for the believer. It's an undeniable, immutable spiritual reality, therefore, think like it and act like it.

As you begin to think according to this new truth (by

---

faith), your experience will eventually begin to change. It might take a day, a week, a month, or a year, but eventually if you think differently, your experience will begin to line up with this spiritual reality that has always been in His Word.

I'm not talking about a faith that produces no results, rather I'm talking about faith that perseveres and stays the course. It eventually, at some point or another *will* produce results.

When I speak of reckoning, I'm not talking about making up something that doesn't exist, I'm speaking of reckoning (considering it to be true) a reality that's already there.

In regard to living in His presence, the reality that we start with is that God lovingly welcomes us. He invites us, and we have been given the rights and privileges as sons of God to enter into this sacred privilege of living in the presence of God.

When I come before the Father, I really am in His presence whether I feel it or not. I acknowledge Him as my Father. I acknowledge my identity as a beloved, righteous son, and I thank Him for His love and His presence regardless of what I do or do not feel in that moment.

This is where the rubber meets the road. I do not

wait to feel the Father's love before I thank Him for it; I reckon it to be so. I declare the truth of the reality of the Father's love for me regardless of my feelings.

I thank Him for His presence when perhaps the only thing I feel is... sleepy or distracted or whatever negative thing. This is what I mean when I say, "by faith."

Sometimes when I minister publicly, and I feel the presence of God in an overwhelming way, as well as others experiencing the manifest presence of God in a way that touches their emotions and even their bodies. Sometimes it can look wild. I find it humorous when I consider how some people will criticize and say all of it is based on emotions. Oh, if they only knew!

A few years ago, I ministered at a pastors' conference in South America at a 6 AM service. I have not been known to be a morning person whatsoever. I had to drag my carcass out of bed at 4 something to get ready for the meeting. There was nothing within me that *felt* anointed, enthusiastic, spiritual, or excited to speak. The only thing I *felt* like doing was staying in bed, but we walk by faith, not according to our feelings.

I released the word of the Lord that morning, and

the Holy Spirit released the joy of the Lord over many people. It was a wonderful time in His presence, but I first had to reckon myself dead to sleep and alive to being awake. Dead to the flesh, and alive to the joy of the Lord which is my strength.

One of the most common things that trip up many believers is focusing on what they don't feel. While I absolutely love the tangible, manifest presence of God, what I can't do is focus on how tangible it is.

If I say I want to enter His presence, but I entirely gauge His presence based on what I don't feel, my focus is still on me. This is a subtle but powerful trap which can distract us. I choose to live in the freedom to focus on my Father and not on my feelings.

I know the truth, and the truth is He is my Father. He loves me, He likes me, He's always there for me, always listening and loving me. That truth will never change. My feelings sure can change, but that truth never does. Only the truth you really know will really set you free.

So, instead of focusing on my feelings (what I do or don't feel), I focus on my Father and His faithfulness which never changes.

Do you remember when you learned how to ride a

bike? At first you were probably really concerned with your balance and the feeling of leaning too far to one side or the other. Once you learned to look ahead and relax, you were able to really take off.

Forget about your feelings and focus on your Father.

Chapter 5

CHOOSE WHAT YOU FOCUS ON

When it comes to entering in to and abiding in the presence of God, we must remember again that we cannot force ourselves or God to give us an experience in His presence. I can't control what God does or doesn't do, but out of a loving, intimate relationship, I can certainly influence Him.

While I can't make God manifest His presence to me, I can make myself focus upon the goodness of God, and thus worship Him and begin to attract His presence. If in seeking to enter God's presence I begin to be aware of the fact that I'm not feeling His presence, that in itself is not a problem as long as I move on and continue to focus on loving Him and beholding Him.

If after becoming aware that I'm not feeling His presence, I instead of continuing to behold Him and love Him, shrink back and become introspective, I will probably forfeit the blessing that the Lord wants to give me because I put my eyes back on myself.

This can be difficult, especially for those of us who are very tuned in to our own feelings. The Holy Spirit wants to teach us how to keep the affections of our heart set upon the Lord even when we don't "feel anything." He doesn't change. Our feelings and emotions may change, but who He is in His love and faithfulness never changes.

This is why the weapon of thanksgiving is so powerful. It redirects our mind and heart from the negative onto the positive. It refocuses our perspective back onto what God has done, rather than what we feel like He hasn't done.

It says in Psalm 100 to enter His gates with thanksgiving. I feel like a lot of us tend to overlook this powerful weapon of thankfulness because of its simplicity. Some of us are incessantly searching for the esoteric key of living in God's presence: seven steps to this, six steps to that, or the revealing of some ancient mystery. All the while God has set before us a simple tool right out in plain sight for us to use every day.

While it might not always be easy, choosing to express thankfulness is not complicated. It's a choice.

Here is what I've discovered. If I'm going through a difficult time, I usually don't feel like giving thanks. Wow! Big revelation, right? But I know I should give thanks even though I don't feel like it. What do I do?

I can feel reluctant to tell God how thankful I am

when I'm internally struggling with a poor attitude. When in reality, what I need to begin to do is to forget about my negative feelings for a moment and begin to express my thanksgiving, begin to declare my gratitude.

What invariably begins to happen is the more I express my gratitude, the more I begin to feel grateful. It might not happen in a moment, it might not be right away, but it will eventually happen.

Why is this? It is because though I might not be able to control what I feel, I *can* determine what I focus on. What I focus on will eventually determine what I feel. Feelings follow focus. If I turn that around and focus on my feelings, I'll be like a dog chasing its tail. I'll just be going around in circles.

It's not that we can't learn many things from our feelings. The Holy Spirit can reveal a lot of things about ourselves to us through what's going on in our emotions. The problem is when I'm ruled by my emotions rather than by truth, I won't see things accurately.

Giving thanks to God (I Thess. 5:18) puts things in proper perspective so that we can see life clearly and hear the voice of the Holy Spirit.

Paul tells us in Philippians to do everything without

grumbling or complaining, and the Word of God is filled with admonitions to give thanks to the Lord. God hates grumbling and complaining (people died in the Old Testament because of it). He's attracted to gratitude.

If you want to hear the voice of God, tune into hope and thanksgiving because the frequency of heaven is hope.

When God commands expressions of thanksgiving and a lifestyle of gratitude, He's not doing it to be cruel, unfeeling, or harsh. It's because He's a good Father who wants what's best for us. He knows that us choosing gratitude is what's best for us.

Every night at the Olson house as we sit around at the dinner table, we pray over the meal, then we go around the table and each share what we are thankful for that day. Why is that? We do it because it's easy to say a quick prayer and "give thanks" then devour the meal without really having thankful hearts. I want us to go around the table and each speak out loud what we are thankful for. Gratitude is a lifestyle that I want my family to cultivate.

I cannot guarantee that by giving thanks to the Lord, you will "feel" His manifest presence. What I can guarantee is that if you do not give Him thanks, you will not be able to live a sustained lifestyle in His manifest presence.

This is why the principle of praise and worship is so powerful. If we truly engage in worship, not just music and singing, we begin to set our hearts and affections on who God is. The beauty of it is that we are conformed to what we focus on. As we begin to gaze upon the beauty of the Lord in our worship, we become like that which we behold. We must choose wisely what we focus on because whatever we focus on will be what we eventually look like. Paul tells us in Colossians 3:1 to set our thoughts and affections on things above, not on things of the Earth. I think some of us at times feel as if, "Well, I could set my affections on heavenly realities if I felt the presence of God."

Again, I love God's presence, I love the peace and joy that His manifest presence brings, but I am not aware of any scripture in the Bible that would command us to experience God's presence. We do have Moses in Exodus telling God that he would rather have His presence than other blessings, but I know of no command in scripture that tells us that we must experience His manifest presence.

You might think, "Well, I thought that's what this book is about: living in God's presence."

Yes, that is what this book is about, and I do believe

we were made to live in God's presence and abide in the reality of His presence with us. But here we have a command by Paul in Colossians 3 that tells us what we should think about and where we should set our affections.

Again, this points us back to this principle: while I can't control God's manifest presence or make Him manifest Himself to me, I can choose my thoughts and determine my affections.

Whether I feel God's presence or not, I can begin to set my mind on things above. What are some of the things that would make up the "things above" that Paul is speaking of?

- The glory of the Lord Jesus Christ,
- the majesty of God and His throne,
- the depth of the Father's love,
- the wonder of the Holy Spirit,
- the throne before which angels and seraphim and cherubim and elders and living creatures bow before Him in worship day and night.

We get to think on these things regardless of whether we feel His presence or not.

As much as I love His presence and would love to experience more of the depth of His presence, I am not left as a victim to the sovereignty of God. I am empowered by a very faithful Father who tells me how to think and what to set my affections upon. This, my friend, is a choice: a choice each of us can make every single day.

As I do what Paul said to do in Colossians 3, set my mind and affections on things above, I start to look like that which I focus on. As we meditate on the glory of Christ Jesus, the beauty of who He is, the sacrificial Lamb who gave His life for us, this King of perfect meekness and matchless majesty, we begin to look more like Him. Our heart attitude begins to take on His character.

As we do this, most often at least a small measure of His presence will begin to come. This is a beautiful pathway into His presence: meditating on who His is.

Even if you don't begin to sense His presence, it is still only right to think about Him and to worship Him. Even if there's no sense of His presence, it is not time wasted because you are training your brain to think on things above and you are strengthening spiritual muscle.

Why is this so important? It's because our natural tendency as human beings, including us as redeemed humanity in Christ, is towards a downward gravitational pull, getting distracted and looking at other things than Christ. We lead busy lives with lots of responsibilities and lots of distractions, and the enemy loves to take advantage of this any way he can.

It can be very tempting to waste our lives sitting around focusing on problems in the world or our own personal weaknesses. You might say, "Are you telling us to ignore the problems in the world."

No, as a matter of fact, I believe we are to create solutions to the problems of the world, but we really can't do it without His presence or without having our hearts fixed on Jesus.

If I'm more overwhelmed by the world's problems, than I am overwhelmed by the love and goodness of God, I really can't be effective in meeting the challenges that those problems pose.

Some may ask, "Are you saying we shouldn't deal with our personal weaknesses?"

No, not at all. What I am saying is that you are not to deal with them alone, without your eyes fixed on Jesus.

Again, what is the strategy of the enemy? It is to do whatever He can to get our eyes off of Jesus. Jesus really wants us to overcome personal weakness and bad habits, but the only way for us to overcome is to keep our eyes fixed on Him and partner with Him on any of our personal problems or problems in the lives of the people around us.

We don't overcome the negative by focusing on the negative; we overcome the negative by focusing on the positive. While we really need to resist sin and say no when temptation comes, the essence of the Christian life is not saying no the devil, it's having a great big YES to Jesus.

It says in James 4:7, *Submit yourselves then to God, resist the devil, and he will flee.* The greater my "yes" in submission to Jesus, the easier my resistance to the devil.

I believe Paul makes this clear as a principle for believers according to Galatians 5:16 which says, *So I say, walk by the Spirit, and you will not gratify the desires of the flesh.*

I would never advocate that we ignore sin, but my main emphasis is to focus on the Savior. We can resist sin and satan as they try to creep up in our lives, all the while keeping our eyes fixed on Jesus by worshiping, loving, and obeying Him with a giant YES to Him in our hearts.

Chapter 6

THE INHERENT POWER OF THE WORD OF GOD

In Matthew 22:29 Jesus rebuked the Pharisees saying, *"You are in error because you do not know the scriptures or the power of God."* NIV

I believe in this passage Jesus is making it clear to us that it is not sufficient to just know the Word of God (the Bible) or to just know the power of God. One without the other is incomplete.

As Leonard Ravenhill used to say, *"It is not enough just to know the Word of God; we must know the God of the Word."*

Unfortunately, much of the church is split up into different camps. Some emphasize only the Word of God, while others overemphasize the power of God to the exclusion of the Word of God.

The Word of God and the power of God are not at odds with each other because the same Holy Spirit who wrote the Book is the one who gives the power.

I want to be very careful what I say here, because it may sound like I'm speaking out of both sides of my mouth.

First of all, let's start off by saying that any long-term

pursuit of His presence without taking advantage of what the Holy Spirit wrote down through men of God of old to give us the cannon of Scripture is simply foolish at best and very dangerous at the worst.

The Word of God is foundational in my life. The more I read it, the more I appreciate it. The more I appreciate it, the more I love and honor the Word of God. It is the measuring rod by which every subjective experience is to be judged.

Scripture itself tells us that the Word of God is eternal. The primary language of the Holy Spirit, the way in which He speaks to us, is the language of Holy Scripture.

Can God speak to us through preachers, podcasts, friends, relatives, our spouse, our own children, movies, television, even this very book? Yes, of course He can. If we're paying attention, we will often hear Him speak through all of these means. But the primary means through which He will speak to us is by His Word.

Even when He speaks to us through other means, it is still all to be judged by His written Word.

This is where we come to the part where I say what I'm about to say with fear and trepidation. Jesus did not die His horrible ugly death being tortured on the cross and shedding His precious blood, just so we could know a book, even the greatest Book ever, God's Word.

He shed His precious blood, so we could be restored back into right relationship with the Father, know Him, be loved by Him, love Him intimately, and glorify Him. The Bible, as amazing and incredibly important as it is, points to Christ Himself. It is not the end in itself. The word of God (Bible) points to the Word of God (Jesus).

You might be thinking right about now, "Wow, I thought this was a good book until now, but now you have entered into heresy. Christopher, you have devalued the Word of God."

Actually, what I want to do is to elevate the Word of God to its proper place, and that is that the Word of God points us to Christ.

See what Jesus Himself said in John 5:37-40 NIV, *"And the Father who sent Me, has Himself testified concerning Me. You have never heard His voice nor seen His form, nor does His Word dwell in you, for you do not believe in the One He sent. You diligently study the Scriptures because you think that by them you possess eternal life. These are the Scriptures that testify about Me, yet you refuse to come to Me to have life."*

Wow! What a rebuke. These men truly studied the Scriptures; Jesus affirmed that. But He still rebuked them because although it was good to diligently study Scripture, the goal of Scripture is to hear His voice and know Him. Instead of knowing Him, seeing His form and knowing His voice, they refused to come to Him.

As Richard Wurmbrand said, "Theology is the word about the word about the word about the Word. Doctrine is the word about the word about the Word. The Bible is the word about the Word, but Jesus is the Word."

Is there anything wrong with Scripture? Is there anything wrong with studying Scripture or memorizing Scripture? No, no, no. A thousand times, no.

But if all we have is Biblical knowledge, yet we do not recognize His voice or know Him, then all we are left with is fruit from the tree of the knowledge of good and evil.

Paul says in 1 Corinthians 8:1, that knowledge puffs up.

Let's be honest about church history. Unfortunately, the wonderful Word of God has been used by many men over the centuries to justify a lot of wicked things, not the least of which has been the killing of other Christ-followers because of someone's wrong interpretation of Scripture. A prime example of this would be the Inquisition, and unfortunately even the persecution of Catholics at the hands of Protestants.

The Word of God tells us that the Bible is a sword, but these are examples of a sword that's being used the wrong way. The Word of God is meant to be used as a weapon in our hands against our enemy the devil, not against our brothers and sisters in Christ.

Obviously, there is a lot more that could be said about wrongly using the Word of God, but let's look at how the Word of God is to be utilized in entering into and abiding in His presence.

Let's look at what Jesus said in John 6:57 NIV, *"Just as the living Father sent Me, and I live because of the Father, so the one who feeds on Me will live because of Me."*

Because of this verse, I am convinced that the primary way in which we are to use the Word of God is as a means to feed on the life of Christ.

There are many different ways to read the Word of God. Sometimes we just read it from cover to cover to familiarize ourselves with the content. This is perfectly fine and necessary because we can't know what it means until we know what it says.

When it comes to devotional reading however, I believe this verse is key. We don't come to the Bible just for mere information. We come to the written Word to encounter the Word of God Himself and to let His Spirit breathe into us the spiritual reality of the written Word.

I remember when I was a kid and would go to our city municipal swimming pool. There was a high diving board. I think it was 200 feet high; at least that's how it seemed to me as a twelve-year-old. In actuality it was probably 15 feet high, I would guess.

The first year or two that I went to that swimming pool, when I was 11 and 12, I never ascended the tall, scary ladder of the diving board. But with slight envy and much curiosity I would often watch others as they ascended the ladder. I eventually worked up enough courage to climb up there myself and take a dive. It was scary and fun all at once.

After that first dive, I kept climbing up and coming back for more. I was hooked.

With all of my experience on the diving board, there's one thing I never saw happen. I never saw people gathering on the diving board, standing around talking about what an amazing board it was while staring at the water from a great distance.

Wouldn't that be ridiculous? A diving board is created so that people can dive from it into the water. It wasn't made merely to be stood on and talked about. It is literally a springboard into an experience.

Many times in the church we say things like, "I'm just standing on the Word." Maybe instead of just standing on the Word, we should dive into the ocean depths of the reality of who God is. We need to allow the Word of God to be the springboard it was created to be by letting the Holy Spirit take us into His presence and the depths of God's heart.

Many of us in the church sadly seem to be content to stand on the diving board of information while there is a glorious ocean of the depths of the love of God waiting for us beneath.

Some do not dive because they've been religiously trained to believe that there's nothing but a board to experience, and that's all they are: bored. Others have heard whispers and rumors of another realm that can be experienced in the ocean of God's love, but they're simply too scared to step off the board.

Often in the church we like to talk about how the Word of God is unchanging. We say that because it's true. It does not change according to the whim or desire of carnal man, sinful appetites, or the ever-murky waters of cultural relativism.

One of the basic ways in which the Word never changes is that it is to always point us to Christ Himself.

When Jesus sacrificed Himself on the cross, He didn't say to us as His bride, "I died and gave my life for you so that you could have a Book and read all about what I used to do and how I used to reveal Myself so you can find out about the intimacy and experiences that other men and woman had which you will never be able to taste of this side of heaven. Good luck with the book. See ya."

No! Thank God He gave us the Holy Spirit who authored the Bible through many men of God. But He didn't just give us the Book; He gave us Himself. We will not be satisfied until we know Him and the fullness of His radiant love, and neither will He.

Chapter 7

HOLINESS: NOT OPTIONAL

I hope that all I have shared so far has been a source of great strength, comfort, and encouragement to inspire you to go deeper with God and further in His presence. At this point, I must clarify an important point and perhaps even give a warning.

My assumption in writing this book is that the people who would take the time to read it are those who are genuinely hungry for God and wanting to experience the fullness of everything that God has for them.

To me, that kind of attitude would necessarily include a life of surrendered obedience to the Lordship of Jesus Christ. I also recognize that there are many people today who speak and teach of encounters with God's presence, but who make no connection with our obedience to the Lord.

I understand that my primary focus needs to be the grace of the Lord Jesus Christ, the goodness of God, and what He has already accomplished for me at the cross. I enter in by grace through faith, not by any legalistic striving, trying to earn something with God. While I affirm this truth, you cannot read the Bible, New Testament included, without recognizing the absolute importance of obedience.

My point is that it is foolish to assume that one can live in the manifest presence of God while living a lifestyle of disobedience, clinging to sin in one's heart. As crazy as it is, unfortunately there are numerous people today who have sought to embrace living in God's presence while also living a lifestyle of compromise and sin.

Sadly, this has been the tragic case for not only a number of believers, but for many leaders in the body of Christ for many years as well. The first thing we need to do is instead of being quick to judge them, is to recognize our susceptibility to deceiving ourselves by evading obedience and holiness and making subtle justifications in our own minds and hearts.

If we are truly honest with ourselves, we've all done this at times, at least in small ways.

Although I love to feel the presence of God (and I really believe He enjoys manifesting His presence to us, and He enjoys the fact that we enjoy His presence) the fact is I can't live by my feelings. I must live by truth. That is why it's so important to spend consistent time reading and meditating on the Word of God.

I have had plenty of times, especially over the last several years, when I've been reading the Word of God, the Holy Spirit whispers to my heart, gives me revelation from His Word, and at times overwhelms me with His presence. As much as I truly love those moments, the reality is I've had more times where I've just simply read the Word and felt NOTHING. That's OK. I don't have to feel anything. I simply need to have the truth of His Word getting into my system.

I'm not one to take vitamins, but I assume those who do take vitamins do not feel an electrical charge of energy when they pop them into their mouth. People understand that getting enough of the right vitamins into our bodies over a long period of time is beneficial to us and helps sustain us over the long haul regardless of what we feel in the moment. It's the same with the Word of God.

There is, on the other hand, one other thing I would like to share that I do experience at times while reading the Bible. What is that, you may ask? It's a good old-fashioned kick in the rear or a startling slap in the face from the Spirit of God as He convicts and challenges me with His Word.

If I'm not in the Word, then the Holy Spirit cannot take His Word and correct me with it. I need to be consistently feeding on the Word of God. That loving slap upside the head that I sometimes feel when I'm reading the Word of God is something I need. It's something you need. It is necessary for all of us.

We can't expect to live in the blessings of His presence while not obeying His Word, and we can't obey His Word if we don't know what it says.

In John 14:15 Jesus says, *"If you love Me, you will obey what I command."* In verse 21a He says, *"Whoever has My commands and obey them, he is the one who loves Me."* In verse 23 He says, *"If anyone loves Me, he will obey My teaching."*

These words alone from Jesus show us the importance of obedience. In verse 23 Jesus goes on to say, *"My Father will love him, and we will come to him and make our home with him."*

We can't enjoy the blessings and benefits of the Father and Son making His home with us if we don't do the first part, and that's to obey Him.

In the very next verse (24a) Jesus says it another way, *"He who does not love Me, will not obey My teaching."* In other words, if I harden my heart to the Lord, and consistently disobey His Word, I demonstrate that I really don't love Him. Our obedience is very important.

You might say, "I thought it was all by grace." It is. It's His grace that teaches us to say no to sin and to obey Him. (Titus 2:12) It is His grace that empowers us, but we must yield ourselves to cooperate with the grace of God.

I think one of the traps that we have fallen into in the body of Christ over the years has been to run to extremes. One extreme says that it's all God and nothing of me. The other extreme says that the entirety of our salvation and sanctification and every benefit of living in the Kingdom is all on us.

Both extremes are not only wrong, but they are dangerous. Yet this is what happens sometimes when we look at theological concepts in a vacuum, devoid of relationship.

Regarding either extreme, if we say that it's all on God or it's all on us, we wind up with only a one-sided relationship. That is really no relationship at all. Is not relationship a partnership? Is not relationship about communication and an exchange of ideas? A giving and taking? Influencing one another?

Some of you might be tempted to say, "Whoa. The difference with this relationship is that He's God, and we're not. Are you trying to say that we influence God?"

Paul tells us in Ephesians 4:30a, *"And do not grieve the Holy Spirit of God."* What's the implication? Our actions or attitudes or disobedience have an effect on God. We are capable of doing things as believers that grieve the Person of the Holy Spirit.

Obviously, the answer is yes. We can influence God. This is simply called relationship. Therefore, my walk with the Lord is not all on me, and it's not all on God. While we clearly need to always emphasize that it is way more on Him, we're completely lost and damned without Him and His grace. Nonetheless, we do have a part to play.

Our part, however small it is, is extremely important. Our obedience matters. Paul says, *For sin shall not be your master, because you are not under law but under grace.* Romans 6:14 NIV

The clear evidence that shows that we haven't received the grace of God in vain, is that we live free from sin and in victorious obedience to the Lord. I don't obey to earn grace; that's impossible. Grace cannot be earned, but my obedience is evidence of grace received.

Chapter 8

CONSUMING CHRIST IN THE WORD

Years ago, I heard John Marquez talk about a menu, and the basic premise of the story has always stuck with me.

I have an amazing, beautiful wife named Beth and four wonderful children. If I were to take them to the best steak house in our state and the host seats us and gives us the menus. And we sit there staring at the menu for fifteen minutes, eventually the server would wonder we when were finally going to be ready to order.

Suppose I tell him, "No, we need a little more time."

He comes back in half an hour and I tell him we're still busy reading the menus, studying them in fact.

Then he returns a while later, and after sitting there for an hour, I still tell him, "No, we still don't' want to order. We're looking at all the nice pictures on the menu. As a matter of fact, we're even studying it in the original Hebrew and Greek!"

After another ten minutes, before the server can come back to ask us again if we want to order, I tell my family what a nice evening it's been looking at the pictures of all the succulent food available. Having studied the menu in the original language, it was now time for us to leave.

So, we hand the menus back to the server, and I march my family out to the van while telling them what a nice time we've had as a family.

At least two results would definitely have occurred. My family would think I'm crazy (the server probably would too), and we would still all be very hungry.

Why is that? Because as good as it is to read a menu and understand its contents, it was never meant to be an end in and of itself. If all you do is study about food but never eat, you'll die of hunger.

Sadly, this is how many Christians live. They're so focused on a menu that is really an invitation to a banqueting table that He has prepared for us. So many seem to be satisfied with just understanding all the nuances of the menu, never diving into the buffet of His presence and love.

When all we do is read the Book instead of feed on His being, we miss the point.

What might this still look like in my life today? I will tell you there are still plenty of times when I am reading the Bible because I love the Bible. There may be several chapters that I want to read. I will often in one sitting, want to read John 14-16, Romans 4-8, along with the Sermon on the Mount, some Psalms, and a Proverb... and an Old Testament story... and Hebrews... and .... I just can't stop. I love the Bible!

This has happened to me numerous times over the last several years. The Holy Spirit has the audacity to rudely interrupt my Bible reading to speak directly to my heart. Can you believe it? It is in those moments that I have to choose between merely memorizing the menu or feeding on the One who is life Himself.

Obviously, God is not as into my Bible reading routine as I am. He actually seems to enjoy interrupting my time in the Word to speak directly to my heart.

It has been a process, but I have had to learn to yield to the presence of God and to the voice of Holy Spirit when He introduces these holy interruptions.

The beautiful thing about it is, is that it's never about contradicting the Word. It's about valuing the Book, but then truly honoring the Author when He Himself shows up on the scene. In those moments, I cannot settle for a religious reading routine. Rather, I must give way to the Lover of my soul.

A number of years ago, I was spending time with the

Lord and reading my favorite chapter of the Bible again: Romans 8. My clear intention was to read the entire chapter from beginning to end, and God knows I really tried.

But as I read the first verse which says, *"Therefore, there is now no condemnation for those who are in Christ Jesus,"* I felt like I needed to read it again. So, I read it again. Then I read it again. Then I felt the Lord lead me to read it yet again. This happened over and over, and I thought that at that rate I wouldn't finish the chapter until the next day.

Yet the Lord kept having me read it over and over again. To my natural mind, it seemed like a pretty ridiculous way to try to read the Bible. But as I continued to read it over and over again, the Holy Spirit led me to personalize it. I began to declare out loud, "There is no condemnation for me – *for me* – FOR ME!"

I soon began to declare that there was not even one little ounce of condemnation directed at me from the heart of the Father. As I began to meditate on the implications of this verse, I began to celebrate this glorious, theological fact: that God, my beloved Father is not in any way, shape, or form condemning me at any moment.

I began to rejoice in the fact that condemnation was

poured on Christ at the cross for me. So, because I'm in Christ, I don't have condemnation. Instead I have Christ's acceptance.

Before I surrendered my life to receive this gift of pardon from sin, I *was* condemned, but *now* I am no longer in Adam. I am in the second Adam: Christ Jesus. He not only bore my sin, but He also bore my condemnation on the cross.

Therefore, Romans 8:1 is the spiritual reality that I, as a child of God, have the privilege of living in every day.

Before I knew it, my voice got louder and louder in great celebration for what Christ accomplished for me at the cross. I just kept declaring Romans 8:1 over and over again. I was not wondering if it was true, not hoping it was true, rather lifting my voice in grateful celebration that this amazing verse refers to me and has been and always will be eternally true.

A huge smile began to spread across my face as joy began to flood my soul. What I received that day was not mere theological information, it was Holy Ghost revelation (based upon His written Word.)

That became so personal to me; it led to personal transformation. I don't believe I ever did finish the rest of Romans chapter 8 that day. I learned to welcome a Holy Spirit interruption when the Author Himself invades the reading of His Book.

A couple of years later, I was at home. I believe it was a Thursday night, I was pacing our bedroom floor while reading the Word of God.

That particular night I was reading Hebrews chapter 10:19, *"Therefore brothers since we have confidence to enter the Most Holy Place by the blood of Jesus."*

I began to also read it in Spanish. *"Tenemos plena libertad para entrar en el Lugar Santisimo."*

For some reason reading it in Spanish made it seem to stand out to me more. I began to be struck by this idea: most of my life the idea of entering the Most Holy Place conjured up images of fear and holy terror. I had always heard stories of the high priest entering with a rope tied to his ankle because they might have to pull out his dead body if he did one thing wrong.

This wasn't like merely entering into a Synagogue or church building, it was entering into the Most Holy Place, the presence of the Most Holy God. You know, the One who in the Old Testament wiped out groups of people and opened up the ground to swallow rebellious, complaining Israelites.

In light of that, the word confidence never came to

my mind when I thought of entering such a place. As my Spanish version puts it: full freedom.

Seeing how the terms confidence and freedom never went along with the idea of entering God's holy presence, what was I to do? I could either cling to my trained religious perceptions or go with the Word of God. But I couldn't hold on to both. Inevitably, I'd have to hold on to just one and let go of the other.

Instead of striving to let go of old perceptions, I just began to repeat over and over what the Word of God had already made clear. I read this passage out loud in both English and Spanish over and over again. I began to thank Him for His invitation to come into His presence, and that in Christ we now have a better, everlasting covenant.

Because of what Jesus did, He made the way for me to come into the Father's holy presence. The suffering He endured in His body and the blood that He shed, give me access. He paid a high price for my free access.

I quickly realized I could not move beyond this verse. As I spoke it out loud over and over in both languages, I began to thank Him that this is reality. That this is eternal truth extended to every believer in the New Covenant. That this glorious invitation of grace is extended to ME.

The more I began to thank Him, the more this truth erupted within my spirit man. The more I thanked Him, the more real it became to me. The more real it became to me, the more I thanked Him. The more I did that, the more joy began to well up on the inside of me.

The joy that erupted on the inside of me did not come because I was pursuing joy. It did not come because I was pursuing a manifestation, an experience, or an emotion. I was simply responding to the truth that was always in His Word.

As I began to mix my faith by thanking Him that it was truth regardless of what I felt or had previously thought, great joy welled up within me and the presence of God began to fall upon me. It was joy unspeakable and full of glory (1 Peter 1:8).

This experience went on for at least a solid hour, probably closer to two. For a long time, I could not stop laughing as His presence kept coming upon me in wave after wave.

At some point in the middle of all of this, my little girl who was probably around 7 years old at the time, heard me and poked her head in the door and asked me, "Daddy, is God tickling you again?"

It was hard in the moment to give a precise theological explanation to her question. So, in the middle of my laughter I just said, "Yes." *

These are just a couple of times where I learned to allow the Holy Spirit to interrupt the reading of His Word, or perhaps it's better stated to say, when He wants to refocus my reading to one single verse because He really wants to highlight it in my spirit.

I have found that it's better to go with the Holy Spirit and not lean on my own understanding. He knows what He's doing when I come before Him to spend time with Him.

*Oftentimes kneeling in reverence towards God is a very appropriate response, especially when He manifests His holiness. The right response to God manifesting His holiness is to fear the Lord and have a reverential response that might even be accompanied with tears at times. God initiates, and we respond. The nature of His character that He is emphasizing in a given moment determines the how we should respond.

Chapter 9

ENCOUNTERING HIS PRESENCE

In this chapter, I would like to share some stories of how God has changed my life. My purpose in sharing these encounters is simply to whet your appetite and for you to believe God for your own encounters. As I have shared these stories while preaching in different parts of the world, many times I have seen God take the power of these testimonies and deeply impact many people with His love and presence.

My prayer is that hunger will be awakened, and you will feel the Holy Spirit drawing you into Papa's presence.

On Sunday, August 25, 2002, my wife and two little kids were in bed. I was hanging out in our living room with the lights off and some quiet worship music gently playing in the background.

I cannot say that I was pursuing the Lord, seeking God, worshipping, or even generally what we would call praying. I was just hanging out and talking to the Lord.

What happened next is very difficult for me to describe. There are just some things that happen that seem to transcend our ability to put into human language. But as poor as my description will be, I will give it a try.

I suddenly realized that Jesus was standing in front of me. I did not see Him with my eyes, but I know it was Him. This was not just the presence of God, but it was Jesus Himself standing right before me.

Though I couldn't see Him, I don't believe that the experience would have been more real had I been able to see Him. I tried to ask the Lord why He was there right in front of me. Before I could finish my question, I realized He was now kneeling down in front of me. He began to wash my feet.

It was beautiful, humbling, surreal, and overwhelming all at once. In spite of how wonderful it was, one of my first reactions was a sense of injustice. I said, "No, Lord, why are You doing this? I should be the one on my knees washing Your feet; Not the other way around."

It was then that He told me, "I'm not just washing your feet; I'm washing your soul."

I knew that He meant that He was washing my identity. He told me, "Christopher, you're not a sinner who struggles to love God. You're a lover of God who resists sin."

I had heard some similar words before from some

teaching. At the time it was a nice concept. Suddenly in His presence, with Jesus kneeling before me washing my feet, I was overwhelmed by His love. Hearing these words come straight from His heart into mine, it was a totally different deal. It was way different from just hearing those words in a teaching.

I immediately knew He wanted to change the way I perceived myself. I could look back over many years and see that I had been a young man who was a sincere Christian who often tried really hard to live for God. But I saw much failure.

The devil, the accuser of the brethren, would often try to define my life by my struggles and my failures, rather than by who I am in Christ. Sadly, I had so often agreed with him to the point that it had become my own perspective of my life.

I was in one moment, getting a glimpse into the Father's perspective of myself and how Jesus Himself defines me. I sat there and wept and wept as He washed over me with waves of His love. It was glorious and overwhelming.

I had never known such a pure, perfect love that was now touching me in the very core of my being. It was truly overwhelming, and all I could do was weep. Eventually that love felt so good, that I began to experience joy. It was truly amazing.

After quite a while, I tried to get up off the couch to walk back to the bedroom. I only made if a few feet when I fell into the recliner because the presence of God was so heavy upon me. I just sat there stuck to the recliner as waves of God's presence and love washed over me.

In a way, it was as if there was no sense of time in His glorious presence. On the other hand, I knew it was very late by this point. It was the early hours of the morning. I thought, "God this is great. This is amazing, but I've got to get some sleep. I can't get out of this recliner. This doesn't seem very practical. I have to teach in the morning. What are You doing?"

It was at that point that He responded and said, "You can't get up. That's good. I've got you right where I want you. I've got you so weighted down with my presence that you can't get up. You are resting in my presence, and you will not be able to get up until I let you up. For years you have tried to minister out of your own understanding, with very little anointing or sense of my presence, and thus with little fruit. Now you are resting here in my presence. You will only be able to get up as I empower you to. But now when you get up and minister, you will minister in the power of my Spirit with my presence upon you, flowing in the anointing."

I then realized that it was not just a momentary accident that I couldn't make it to the bedroom and ended up in the recliner instead. He was showing me how it prophetically represented the lifestyle He wanted me to begin living.

The new lifestyle was to be that I could not minister and give to others until I first rested in His presence. Only then would there be an overflow of the Spirit that could produce real fruit.

After he spoke these things to me, I just laid there allowing myself to be submerged in His love and presence and allowing Him to do whatever He wanted to do in me.

After a while, more joy began to flood my soul. I don't remember what time it was, but eventually I was able to make it to bed in the early hours of the morning.

The next morning when I went to teach the Bible class, I discovered I couldn't teach. I opened in prayer, and all I could do was pray and weep. I was undone.

Over the next few years, I found it very difficult to

speak of this experience as it was so personal and deeply intimate. On the few occasions I did try to share it, I usually couldn't make it very far without crying.

Since that time, I've had many wonderful experiences with the Lord where He's taken me deeper into His presence and love. But I still have to say that I've never before or since had an encounter like that one on the night of August 25, 2002. I'm so grateful for His mercy and grace.

Chapter 10

GUILT, CONDEMNATION, AND THE BLOOD

Ephesians 3:12 tells us to come before the Lord with freedom and confidence. Guilt, condemnation, and shame are the opposites of freedom and confidence. It's impossible to come before God in true freedom and confidence with any measure of boldness if we're still being held captive by the lies of the enemy, bound by guilt, condemnation, and shame.

There are many sincere believers who long to live in the Lord's presence, but between the accuser of the brethren himself, and their guilty consciences, they have a hard time approaching His presence, let alone living there.

Our conscience is a powerful thing. It is a beautiful tool that God has given us meant to help and protect us, but it is also something that the enemy loves to take advantage of.

The word conscience is a compound word: 'con' meaning with; 'science' meaning knowledge. The conscience is like the law. It can show us where we've gone wrong and make us feel bad, but it cannot save us. The best that it can do is point us to

Christ. In and of itself, it cannot save us. (Gal. 3:24)

If we solely depend upon our conscience (with our understanding of knowledge) we can end up eating from the tree of the knowledge of good and evil rather than the tree of life.

Paul said knowledge puffs up (1 Corinthians 8:1). So, knowledge, or our conscience, is a good thing, but like the law, by itself is completely insufficient. It can tell us when we've done something wrong and leave us feeling guilty for our sin.

Unfortunately, some Christians, thankfully not many, ascribe to a theology that believes the guiltier we feel, the better. It is right for us to feel horribly guilty for sins we have not repented of, but true repentance should lead to the freedom from guilt. We were never made to live with a guilty conscience.

We might feel the sting of a guilty conscience on occasion, which should only point us back to Christ. After having repented, we are cleansed not only from the sin itself, but from the guilt that comes with it.

Do you remember ever feeling guilty before you got saved? Do you remember your conscience bothering you before you got saved? Was it a good thing? Probably so, but did it transform your life? No. The best it could do was let you know how much you needed Jesus. That is the purpose of the law.

We've already said how conscience means with knowledge, but for the new covenant believer, the question becomes what kind of knowledge do you have? If all you have is the knowledge between right and wrong, then you're no better off than someone who doesn't know the truth of the gospel.

The knowledge that we as new covenant believers need to possess is more than the knowledge between right and wrong. We must possess the understanding of the power of the blood of Jesus to cleanse us from a guilty conscience.

We know that sin separates us from God, but in this case, I'm not talking about sin in and of itself. I'm going to assume that most of the people reading this book sincerely want to honor God with their lives and live in His presence.

Can you think of a time when you hurt someone or sinned against them and they genuinely forgave you, but you still felt uncomfortable around them afterwards? Maybe it was when you were young and disobeyed your parents. Or maybe you really wounded your spouse and couldn't feel comfortable around them for quite some time even though they said they forgave you.

We are often this way with God. What makes us uncomfortable at times in His presence or keeps us from entering His presence is not the sin itself, but rather the sense of guilt that still lingers.

There are many in the body of Christ who have repented multiple times for sins they committed more than twenty years ago but are still living with a guilty conscience. If you feel uncomfortable with God because of a guilty conscience, why would you even want to live in His presence, if you're convinced He's mad at you?

Guilt and shame are similar but are not synonymous. Guilt can make us feel bad for our actions; shame makes us feel bad simply for who we are. If we've committed a wrong action, we need to feel guilty, so we can repent of it and move on to living free. Shame says that it's not merely what we've done that it wrong; who we are is wrong. Shame takes the guilt associated with sin and attaches it to our identity. It creates an inner turmoil that battles within us.

On one hand, we have a guilty conscience telling us that because of our guilt we're not worthy to be in His presence. That lie is empowered by the accuser of the brethren (Revelation 12:10). On the other hand, we have the Holy Spirit telling us that we're forgiven and clean. The blood of Jesus makes us worthy to be in His presence. The righteousness of Christ now becomes our righteousness and qualifies us to live in the Father's presence (2 Corinthians 5:21).

The truth is once we've repented and put our faith in Christ, the Father completely forgives us. Romans 8:1 says there is now no condemnation for those who are in Christ Jesus. You might say, "Well, I'm in Christ, and I still feel condemned." My question becomes, is that verse a lie? Is Romans 8:1 a contradiction?

On one hand, we have the word of God telling us that for those who are in Christ Jesus there is no condemnation. On the other hand, we have our Christian experience that tells us that we've experienced condemnation since we got saved.

I want to state emphatically that Romans 8:1 *is* a contradiction. It *is* contradicting your emotions and feelings, and it contradicts your experience. When there seems to be a contradiction between the simple truth of God's Word and your own experience, go with the truth of God's Word!

You might say, but that still doesn't solve it for me. I

still really feel guilty; I still really struggle with condemnation. I'm not saying that you don't. Those feelings are very real. The only problem is those very *real* feelings are not based on reality.

We still feel guilty and condemned because of our conscience and because of the devil, who is the enemy of our souls, coming to us as the accuser of the brethren. He is the source of the condemnation, not the Father.

I wish I could say that I know all this is true merely from books I've read and people I've counseled. Mainly I know it's true because of my own life experience.

Paul tells us there is NO condemnation, not even a little bit, from the Father towards those of us who are in Christ Jesus.

My question to you is not whether you've screwed up and committed sin. My question to you is are you in Christ Jesus? Have you repented of your sin? If your answer is yes, then there is no condemnation for you.

We empower what we believe. If we believe a lie, we empower the father of lies. When we agree with the truth, we empower the Holy Spirit in our lives, who is the Spirit of Truth.

The Father's desire and plan is never for us to shrink back in the shadows of shame. Rather it is to boldly come before Him as righteous, holy, joy filled sons and daughters whose guilty consciences have been cleansed by the blood of Jesus and who know their place in the Father's heart.

Going back to the verse we started off with at the beginning of the chapter, Paul tells us to approach God with freedom and confidence. We can't do it while simultaneously living in the shadow of guilt and shame.

Jesus didn't just die to deliver us from sin, but also from all the guilt and shame associated with that sin. Approaching the presence of God in freedom and confidence is our rich inheritance in Christ. Living in freedom and confidence is the privileged lifestyle of every new covenant son and daughter.

Are you living in freedom and confidence? Hopefully you are. If not, I want you to know that you can.

Chapter 11

CARRYING HIS PRESENCE

In October of 2002, about six weeks after I had that powerful encounter with God in my living room that I told you about in chapter 8, I went to a conference in Canada. While I was there, I was blown away by what I saw God doing along with the reports of what I heard He was doing among the nations.

I was powerfully impacted by the presence of God that was so strong there. In fact, during one of the afternoon workshops I could not even make my way back to the hotel room because the presence of God was so strong on me. It made it difficult to walk. I foolishly even tried to call home while in that condition. My wife answered the phone, but I could barely speak. I had never been so powerfully touched by the Lord in a public meeting before. It was so intense.

I flew home on the Sunday following the conference and was scheduled to share that Sunday night at our church.

That Sunday night I got up and tried to share about my experiences at the conference, but I was quite sleep deprived by that point and did not do a good job speaking. But when I simply invited the presence of the Holy Spirit to come and those who were hungry to come up to the front, the presence of God fell in the church.

Immediately the front of the sanctuary altar area was filled with hungry people. We knew that the atmosphere was charged with His presence.

At that time, I did not know how to release the anointing. I just knew how to hunger for Him, and He came and filled the atmosphere.

I didn't know how to give away what I had received. I didn't know how to impart what I had experienced as I was just learning how to receive for myself.

I distinctly remember standing there, seeing all these hungry people. Some of them were kneeling, others crying or lifting their hands. Some were even reconciling with family members. I thought it was amazing, but I didn't know what to do with it.

In spite of the fact that we didn't know what to do with it, it was a great starting point for myself and our church.

Though I had been in similar services like the ones at the conference before, I had never experienced anything like I did at this event. I believe the encounter I had in my living room six weeks earlier set me up to be able to receive from the Lord in a whole new way.

A few months later, I went to a conference in Kansas City, Missouri. The first night I was at the conference, at the end of the service, the evangelist said, "I'm not going to stick around pray for people. I'm just going to say a general prayer over the crowd before I leave."

As I was standing there in the middle of a crowd of a few thousand people, I could feel just a little bit of the presence of God begin to drop in on me as he prayed over the whole place. It was very faint, but it was enough that I could recognize that God was doing something. I realized that I needed to respond to what He was doing. I had to make my way up front to receive prayer.

The evangelist had mentioned that there would be a small prayer team up front available to pray with people. I had to fight my way through the crowd because most everyone in the huge crowd people was leaving since the big-name evangelist wasn't sticking around.

I stood up front and began to wait on the Lord. After a few minutes, I got down on my knees and was crying in God's presence. Eventually someone from the prayer team, to this day I have no idea who, came by and gently put their hand on my head as I was trying to stand back up front the kneeling position. They simply said, "Drink Him in."

At that point I started to fall over. I laid there on a cold cement floor under the weight of God's presence. It was the last day of February 2003. There was no carpet; just cold, hard cement.

As I laid there, the Lord asked me a question. He said, "Are you ready to experience the real pleasure from heaven?"

The idea was that earthly pleasures cannot truly satisfy. For some reason He asked me it a second time. Before I could answer, it was as if something erupted inside of my belly. With such euphoric pleasure, I began to laugh and laugh and laugh.

While all of this was going on, my head was up against the high heel of a woman standing near me. There were only a few of us up front receiving prayer. As far as I could tell, I was the *only* one in this multitude of people making such sounds. Talk about awkward, but I didn't care. It was so amazing. I had never known such pleasure in my whole life.

Another interesting aspect to all of this was that I had been in plenty of meetings over the years where I had seen people laughing. Several years before this, my reaction to the laughter was that it probably wasn't from God. Later on, I thought that it might be from God, but it was just a touch that immature people needed. I certainly didn't need it. I wanted to be a holy man of God. I didn't think I had any need for such foolishness.

So now, there I found myself on the floor doing the very thing I had judged others for doing. In the midst of this ecstatic state of Holy Spirit euphoria, I was simultaneously repenting in my heart for having judged what the Holy Spirit was doing in the lives of others.

Eventually, my brother John and my friend Steve had to help me up. Almost everyone had left, and the janitors had to clean the place, so it could be used for the service the next morning.

The guys gently helped me to my feet. I was able to walk, but only very slowly. By the time we exited the large building, and got to the street in downtown Kansas City, I quickly recognized that I would never be able to walk fast enough to cross the street with all of the thick traffic. The light would stop the cars for a moment, but it wouldn't be long enough for me to make it across.

Because my brother recognized my impaired walking ability, he decided to carry me. He threw me over his shoulder, and carried me across the street, through the parking lot, and dumped me in the car. As he finally dropped me into my seat, I remember thinking, "I don't care if I get hit by a car. I don't care if the whole world hates me. I love everyone. This is amazing."

Mind you, I have never touched a drop of alcohol in my entire life, but in that moment, I was clearly intoxicated by the pleasure of God's love.

After I got home from the conference, I was so hungry to get alone with the Lord. I just wanted to be with Him and to worship Him. To my amazement, His presence kept coming.

I was beginning to experience His manifest presence on a regular basis when I would come before Him. It was wonderful, and I was so hungry for more. At the same time, I had this fear in the back of my mind. It was a nagging question of how long this new sense of His presence would last.

One day as I spent time in prayer and worship, His presence came in such a sweet way. I could really feel the anointing of the Holy Spirit coming upon me. I thought to myself, "Wow, I can really feel the anointing. In the next day or so, when I go to lead worship or do any kind of public ministry, it's going to be really great because I can feel His anointing on me."

As soon as I thought that, I felt the Lord lovingly rebuke me. He said, "Do you think that's why I show up with my presence? Do you think that's why I come to visit you? Just to anoint you for public ministry? Just so I can *use* you? I come to you with my presence and visit you because I love you. I want a relationship with you, not just to use you publicly."

As I kept spending more and more time in His presence in the ensuing weeks, I was wondering if this anointing and the nearness of His presence, the sweet place of intimacy would wear off.

The Lord spoke something very clear and direct to my heart. I have never forgotten it. He said, "Christopher, I'm giving you an inexhaustible anointing."

This put my heart at ease and helped me to recognize that I didn't have to strive and live in fear of losing that clear sense of my Father's love. I could just abide in His love and rest in His presence. He would be there with me and for me.

Chapter 12

RELEASING HIS PRESENCE

Some weeks after I got home from the conference in Kansas City, I received in the mail a couple of video tapes that I had ordered from the conference.

On a Sunday afternoon while my little ones were taking a nap, my wife and I were in our living room watching one of the videos. Somewhere in the middle of watching the video, my wife said something to me that really surprised me. She said, "That must have been a really powerful conference because I can feel the anointing coming off the TV screen."

I was not used to my wife talking like that. I said, "Yes, it was powerful."

Then she said something that really shocked me. She asked if I would pray for her, as if she expected God to tangibly minister to her. This was not a common request from her. I wasn't sure what to do because you see, up until that time, I had been in full time ministry for many years. I knew how to pray nice, kind, usually theologically sound, and sometimes passionate prayers. But there was never a release of power.

I'm not saying that in an intercessory way God

wasn't working behind the scenes in ways I didn't know about when I prayed. But there was never any tangible sense of power released when I prayed for anybody. I was fairly good at the rhetoric of prayer but flowing in the power of the Holy Spirit always seemed elusive to me.

There I was with my wife asking me to pray for her. I had to say something. So, I did what any godly husband would do; I stalled for time.

I told her, "Let's finish the video first." When the video was over, I told her we should put on some worship music. Then when the music was done playing, I said we should wait on the Lord for a little bit. I kept looking for ways to delay the inevitable.

Why? Because I could tell that she had an expectation that God was going to touch her. But I knew that nothing happened to people when I prayed for them.

At that point, I did not know how to release the anointing or the manifest presence of God on anyone else. I was just learning how to drink of the presence of God myself. I was in this season of getting acclimated to His presence, learning how to drink of Him. I did not yet know how to release Him to others.

I sat on the floor next to the couch my wife was lying on. My theory at the time was that although I didn't know how to release the presence of God on others, maybe I could just get close to her and drink of His presence. Then as I would drink of Him, His presence would come on me. Maybe if I was close enough, some of it would overflow to her. That was all that I knew to do at that time.

At that point, having drunk of His presence I finally laid my hands on my wife and began to pray for her. It wasn't just prayer like asking for something. I found myself declaring over her with boldness and authority. My own ears were surprised to hear strong words with a prophetic edge coming out of my mouth.

As the presence of God descended on us, I realized that my wife was shaking under the power of God as she lay on the couch. When I was done and backed away, I saw how she was so visibly touched by the presence of God. I was so shocked and realized that I hadn't just received a nice, little touch from the Lord. It was more than a touch; it was the beginning of a transformation.

That began a season for us that we refer to as the spring of His presence. All of that spring, God's presence kept showing up in our home over and over again in a most wonderful way.

I remember my wife and I lying in bed at times during that season, whispering to one another, "He's here." Even as we laid in our bed at night, the manifest presence of God hovered over us.

Times during this season of His presence were marked by fasting, other times by great joy, and still other times by weeping because of His closeness. Overall, it was marked by being overwhelmed at being so loved by a holy God who drew near.

As amazing as that season was, while I experienced His presence in an overwhelming way in my personal life, we weren't yet experiencing it corporately as a church. Mind you, good things were happening. A deep hunger was being awakened along with a lot of intercessory prayer and fasting. God's presence came in a certain measure, but not in the same way as it did in our home.

One Saturday during this spring of His visitation, our little ones were taking their naps and my wife left for a little while to go grocery shopping. I went into our bedroom as closed the door. As soon as I closed the bedroom door, the presence of God began to come. I just got on the floor to worship Him and be in His presence. It was a wonderful time of worship and mutual exchange of love and affection with my

Lord.

In the midst of this, all of the sudden I began to see something. I saw an image of a gal from our church. I didn't know her name, but I knew she was from our church. The Lord told me that she was hungrier for God than what she knew. It felt as if God wanted to reveal to her how much He was attracted to her heart because she had been accused and condemned by the enemy, and she doubted the sincerity and purity of her own heart. I knew I was to pray for her at church that night.

This was interesting because I didn't normally pray for people at our church at that time. I was a volunteer worship leader at the church in those days, but I wasn't on staff or on the prayer team.

At the end of the service that night, we had a missionary's wife leading the music for the ministry time. This meant that I was free to pray for some people. Again, at that time I did not know how to release the anointing. I was still in the early stages of learning how to drink of the Spirit of God for myself.

I found the gal who the Lord showed me in the vision and shared with her what the Lord had showed me and spoken to me about her. Then I asked if I could pray for her. She agreed readily.

As I stood in front of her, I again realized that I really didn't know how to release the anointing. So, I decided to just drink of His Sprit, and I felt His presence come upon me. After doing that for a minute or two, I reached out my hand to bless her. Before I could touch her forehead, boom, down to the floor she went as we were both overwhelmed by the presence of God.

A very similar thing happened with one or two other people that night as well when I ministered to them. I remember walking out of church slowly late that night under the intoxicating sense of His presence. I was thinking this thought, "Wow, finally I'm experiencing at church what I've been experiencing for a while now at home."

I later on began to realize that the way many Christians live is experiencing something of God at church, but then going back home to stress and striving with little sense of His presence. They feel that they have to get back to church to experience His presence again, when really this is backwards.

As a New Covenant son, I'm the temple of the Holy Spirit and I have access to His presence 24/7. I've been given the privilege of drinking of His Spirit and abiding in Christ all week long. When I do go to a church meeting, hopefully I've been spending time with God all throughout the week, abiding in His love and presence. Therefore, I can just overflow and give to others. I can bless and encourage others without having to worry about whether I "got anything out of" the worship or preaching.

All these years later, I still look back at that time in my life as the season when God invaded with His presence and changed me. So much of my life and ministry today flows out of what God did in me during that season. Before we experienced an outpouring of His Spirit in our church, I first experienced it in my own home.

During that time and over the next several years, I would personally march through every room in my home inviting the Holy Spirit's presence and the reign of Jesus Christ into my house.

We also did this several times as a family. We would do a march for Jesus in our own home with worship music blaring. The children were just toddlers, but as a family we would march through the house making declarations, inviting His presence into our home.

That faith-filled, joyful procession might've looked silly, but I believe God delighted in it and the Holy Spirit took our request seriously.

We've had many meetings in our home since that time where we've seen people powerfully touched by the manifest presence of God. It's like the Holy Spirit just loves our house.

I invite you to do what we did. Welcome the Holy Spirit into your home. He is eagerly looking for a place to land. May He find a resting place in your life.

Chapter 13

WHAT DOES GOD REALLY THINK ABOUT YOU?

Some people, even Christians, are somehow sadly convinced that God rarely thinks of them. But what does the truth of God's Scripture say?

How precious are Your thoughts about me, oh God. They cannot be numbered! I can't even count them; they outnumber the grains of the sand! And when I wake up, You are still with me! Psalm 139:17-18 NLT

Wow! This is amazing. The Psalmist tells us that God's thoughts about us are more than the grains of sand. They cannot be numbered. Just think of how many grains of sand are on the beach or in the lake nearest to you. Then think of that for your entire state. Then think of that for the entire west coast of the United States... thousands and thousands of miles of coast line. How many grains of sand would that be? Now add that with all the grains of sand on the east coast as well. That's only one nation, let alone all the beaches and oceans of the world.

The Psalmist says that these God thoughts are more than the grains of sand. We don't know exactly how many thoughts God has about us, but I think it's pretty safe to say that He has billions and billions.

This is either good news or bad news depending on God's attitude toward us, depending the content of His thoughts. If the almighty God of the universe has negative thoughts towards us, that's a bummer. It's one thing for a mere mortal to think negatively about me, but if the sovereign God of all that is, who knows me perfectly inside and out, is thinking poorly of me, I have a good reason to feel depressed.

The question then becomes, what kind of thoughts does God have toward you? Let's look at a verse that many of us are very familiar with.

For I know the thoughts that I think toward you, saith the Lord, thoughts of peace, and not of evil, to give you an expected end. Jeremiah 29:11 KJV

This verse was written by the Holy Spirit through the prophet Jeremiah to God's people while they were in captivity still reaping the consequences of their sinful actions. In this context, God tells us the kind of thoughts that He has toward His people. They are thoughts of peace. They are not evil thoughts. They are good thoughts. Most versions instead of saying an "expected end" translate it "hope."

God, your Father, is filled with precious, wonderful, kind and loving, hope-filled thoughts about you. Remember, He has *billions* of those kinds of thoughts about you!

I would like to now ask you a question. Who does God love more, you or Jesus? Perhaps, before we answer that question we should ask how much does God the Father love Jesus the Son? Is it a little bit, a lot, or with absolute infinite, perfect, extravagant love beyond what we can even imagine? I think the answer is the latter.

But is it even remotely possible that God could love us anything at all like He loves Jesus? Let's see what the Word of God has to say about this.

I am in them and You are in Me. May they experience such perfect unity that the world will know that You sent Me and that You love them as much as You love Me. John 17:23 NLT

Then the answer is YES! Jesus makes it very clear in this passage that God the Father loves us, His children just the same as He loves Jesus. There is absolutely no difference between God's love for Jesus and His love for us. That is amazing!

I want to encourage you right now to meditate on this truth of God's love for you. Right now, say out loud, "Father, thank You that You love me *just* like you love Jesus. Papa God, thank You so much that there is no difference between Your love for Jesus and Your love for me. Thank You that You love me just the same."

Now take a moment of silence to just breathe those words in. Then speak them out one more time.

"Father, thank You that You love me *just* like you love Jesus. Papa God, thank You so much that there is no difference between Your love for Jesus and Your love for me. Thank You that You love me just the same."

How does that feel? Isn't His love amazing! Don't wait to feel God's love to thank Him for His love. Thank Him for His love regardless of what you feel because you truly are loved by Him.

It is wonderful to simply whisper those words to Him as you go throughout your day, thanking Him for His love. It's also wonderful when you're alone with Him, to not just whisper it but to shout it out with gratitude for His great love!

Many times, I have found that as I simply thank Him for His love, His presence begins to just come. When that happens, the more I thank Him, the more I can feel His presence begin to flow. But even if I don't sense His presence, it's wonderful to simply thank Him and confirm this truth over and over again in my mind and heart.

One of the foundational keys to entering God's presence is simply using the tool of worship that He has given us. Psalm 22 says that God inhabits the praise of His people. I always encourage people, when they don't know what else to do, simply to praise and worship Him. But did you know that when we worship Him, it is not just us singing to Him? He also sings over us!

Zephaniah 3:17 says, *The LORD your God is with you, the Mighty Warrior who saves. He will take great delight in you; in His love He will no longer rebuke you but will rejoice over you with singing.*

Wow! What a passage! What a revelation of God's heart toward you! He is not an angry Master tolerating you. He is a loving Father celebrating you. You are His child, and He delights in you!

As a matter of fact, He delights in you so much that He can't contain Himself. He must burst forth in to song as He sings over you!

Sometimes we have a tendency to think that we have to do a lot of things to get God's attention when in reality, as His children, we've had His loving attention from the very beginning. He not only notices you, He lovingly delights in you. That means He takes pleasure in you. You bring Him joy.

A few years ago, I was in the balcony of our church praying. The Lord spoke something very precious to my heart. He told me, "Christopher, every day I sing over you. Whether you are listening to My song or not, I still sing over you. As a matter of fact, I write a new song for you each day. I love it when you pay attention to what I'm singing over you, but even if you were so distracted and ignored My voice every day, it could never stop Me from singing over you."

Ephesians 1:5 tells us that Papa God adopted us in Christ because it was His pleasure to do so. I don't think that just means that God is sovereign and can do whatever He pleases, but it also means He chose you and takes pleasure in choosing you.

One of the most important things to always remember about spending time with the Lord is that the moment you turn your heart to Him to engage His presence, His heart has already been turned toward you.

When you wake up in the morning and begin to spend time with the Lord, remember that even while you were asleep all night, He was still thinking about you and couldn't wait for you to wake up, so you could meet with Him. His heart is for you and is wildly in love with you!

Paul says in Ephesians 1:4a NIV, *For He chose us in*

Him before the creation of the world. Before I comment anything on this verse, let me say up front that I'm not a Calvinist, which is fine, neither is Jesus. So, I'm in good company.

I believe this verse speaks of mysteries that we cannot fully comprehend. Nonetheless, this says that we were chosen in Christ before the foundation of the world. Before when? Before you could do anything right, before you could ever sin or screw up or make a huge mess of things. Before you could ever do anything wonderful or fail miserably, you were chosen before your parents could ever decide whether they liked or wanted you. You were chosen by the Father before any authority figure could ever wound, hurt, or abuse you. You were chosen.

Often times in church we say things like *your past doesn't define you.* I understand why we say these things, but a few years ago I felt like the Lord told me, *Christopher, your past does define you because you're past is not about how you screwed up last week or last year. It's not about whether you were rejected in sixth grade or somebody wounded you years ago. Your past goes all the way back to the cross and even to before the world was made because I chose you all the way back then.*

Why did He choose us? It would be easy to just

state theologically that it's a mystery of the sovereignty of His will. While I completely understand that answer, ultimately, I have to say the reason He chose us is because He wanted us. Nothing or no one made Him choose us against His will. If God chose us, it's because He wanted us.

I'm not saying there are not real experiences of pain, heartbreak, and rejection that we go through, but what I *am* saying is that before we could ever fail or anyone else could fail us, God chose us. His acceptance is much bigger and more powerful than anyone else's rejection.

Our past goes back to the beginning before the creation of the world when we were lovingly chosen and wanted by the Father in Christ. *That* is the only kind of past that is allowed to define us.

Chapter 14

BUILDING SPIRITUAL MUSCLE MEMORY

1 Peter 4:7 says, *"The end of all things is near. Therefore, be clear minded and self-controlled so that you can pray."*

Different versions translate this verse differently, but the Berean Study Bible and the Berean Literal Bible both also say *clear minded.* Notice that Peter tells us to be *clear minded* not *empty minded.* Emptying one's mind would fit more along the lines of eastern meditative practices.

The Christian recognizes that the goal of life is not to be empty of self, but to be truly filled with Christ and His Holy Spirit. We never want to empty ourselves in such a way that attracts the demonic. We want to live a life of clear intentionality in pursuit of the Lord Jesus Christ.

Therefore, Peter tells us not to be *empty minded,* but to be *clear minded* with the implication of our thoughts being set on the Lord. Many of us have felt such a desire to pray, worship, or simply spend time in God's presence, but after a few minutes we get worn out. Why is that?

Well, there could be a lot of reasons for it, but one

of the most basic reasons that all of us have run into is that we find our mind wandering. We start off something like this: God I love You. I just love You, Jesus. I want to worship You and enjoy Your presence. I wonder if we should have green beans with dinner tonight? Lord, I worship You. You're so holy. You're so worthy. You're so good. Did I pay the light bill last week? I sure hope so. That would be really bad if I didn't. I'm sorry, Lord. Please forgive me. I got distracted. God, I love You. I hunger for You. There's nothing I want more than You! I wonder if my team is going to win tomorrow. I sure hope they do. If they can just win this game, they have a great chance at the play-offs. That'd be cool. I wonder if I could get tickets to the play-offs? Maybe I could even invite some friends to the game... Whoa! What happened, Lord? Sorry about that. I really do love You!

Ever been there?

This is why Peter tells us that one of the keys to praying is to have a clear mind. When we are born again, we receive the Holy Spirit into our spirit which produces union with Christ. We are a brand-new creation. Hallelujah! But our minds can still wander when what really want to do is live in wonder.

What is the problem? Or better yet what is the

solution? The answer is to get your mind caught up to where your spirit is at. As a matter of fact, Paul tells us in Romans 12 that a key to transforming your life is to renew your mind.

It's one thing to feel the presence of God on Sunday morning in corporate worship, love the preaching or teaching of the Word at church, be touched by an anointed message at a conference, encounter the Lord powerfully at a revival service, or to... *squirrel!* Oops, there I go getting distracted again.

In other words, it's one thing to receive a blessing from someone else or the environment that they have created, but it's a lot harder to practice self-discipline and train your brain.

One of the foundational aspects of physically working out is pushing through the difficulty and enduring the process of retraining your muscles. There is a similar principle between physically working out and spiritually working out.

Many people take a look at their lives and see that they're all out of shape physically or spiritually. After looking in the mirror, they suddenly get motivated to make the change they know they need to make. They watch something online that tells them how obesity will kill them and much of the food they eat is poison to their body. They jump off the couch, throw away their chips and candy bars, and grab their phone to order the newest treadmill with the touch of a button.

Similarly, they hear a powerful message on holiness, the presence of God, and the need for prayer in their life. They rush down to the front of the church, kneel at the altar, and shed lots of tears. They go home and quickly throw out some sinful things that the Holy Spirit convicted them about. They are now ready for a committed life of prayer, living in God's presence.

The excitement builds over the next few days as they eagerly await the arrival of the new treadmill. After it finally arrives, and they get it all set up, the hard work of developing new muscle memory begins. Their body aches after having been sedentary and overweight for so many years. Suddenly they realize that the excitement about getting the new machine was a lot greater than the excitement of actually doing the work of exercising on the machine.

A few days earlier, they were dreaming of being fit and trim, getting exercise and no longer poisoning themselves. They dreamt of having a healthy body and no longer living with regret. Now all they can think of is how they want to stop their body from aching and how good a triple fudge extreme chocolate five-gallon bucket of ice-cream would taste.

What they fail to realize is that if they will endure for a few more weeks, their mind and body will get adjusted to a new and better reality. So, it is with the one who seeks the path of prayer and a life full of His presence.

When we persevere in prayer even when we don't feel anything, we build our spiritual muscles. In a way we build new muscle memory in our spirit. You can read all the books on prayer and attend all the conferences that emphasize prayer, but there's nothing like just getting in there and doing it. There's nothing like just getting alone with God and saying, "Father, here I am to be with You."

I've never known of anyone to lose weight merely because they sat on a couch for hours day after day reading books about exercise. It's great to read books to get the needed knowledge (hopefully you're being greatly blessed by this one), but at the end of the day there's nothing like just getting in there and doing it.

I remember when I was in my early twenties, I had a strong desire to get alone with God and be in His presence. I would set aside a few hours and shut myself in a room to be with Him. I would tell myself that I wasn't coming out until I'd truly met with Him. I would have my Bible and sometimes worship music with me. I would express my worship to Him, telling Him how thankful I was for His goodness in my life.

Inevitably, I would be distracted with something. I would realize my mind had wandered and quickly pull it back onto the Lord. If there was something very important that I remembered and just could not afford to forget, I would write it down to deal with later. I would immediately begin to express my worship to Him again, not giving up no matter how many times I got distracted or felt like my heart was not connecting.

The point is that I was determined to do whatever it took to give myself fully to Him. I had to press through the discomfort while I painfully produced new muscle memory in my spirit man.

Paul tells us in Galatians 5 that one of the fruits of the Spirit is self-control. There are a lot of things we could say about our need for self-control in so many areas of our lives, but one of the areas that needs self-control the most is our thought life. We must learn that we do not have to accept every thought that pops into our head or of course follow and obey the thought. We have a choice, and God has given us the ability to walk in self-control.

Church history is full of men and women of God who the Lord has used mightily. They learned to overcome the boredom barrier and lavish their worship on Jesus.

You really can retrain your brain by pressing past all of the distractions and the boredom barrier, resulting in a breakthrough of glorious communion with Christ.

Chapter 15

A CLEAR MINDED THOUGHT LIFE

Therefore, I urge you, brothers, in view of God's mercy, to offer your bodies as living sacrifices, holy and pleasing to God – this is your spiritual act of worship. Romans 12:2

There has been a considerable amount of teaching in the body of Christ on the need for us as believers to have our minds renewed. I believe the reason why there's been such an emphasis on it is because that emphasis is something the Holy Spirit has brought about. It is a subject that is dear to my heart, as well as my mind.

While it is only right that we should put a major emphasis on the need to renew our minds, we must not forget what Paul says just before that. He instructs us to no longer be conformed to the pattern of this world.

What are some of the patterns of this world? They are too numerable for an exhaustive list, but here are a few.

- Self-centeredness
- Pride
- Greed

- Lust
- Envy
- Jealousy
- Sexual Immorality
- Rebellion
- Hatred
- Resentment
- Unforgiveness

When we come before the Father to spend time with Him, we want our minds to be in the right place. Based on what Paul tells us in Romans 12:2, before we can fully embrace the renewal of our minds, we must make a break from old sinful, worldly patterns of thinking.

We were all born with sinful, worldly, self-centered patterns of thinking that were then reinforced by the sinful culture around us. The question is not whether we've had wrong patterns of thinking, because we all have. The question is what are we doing to overcome and no longer reinforce, but replace those wrong thought patterns?

At the risk of sounding what some would interpret as legalistic, I must at this point say that we must be very careful with entertainment. We need to learn to pay attention to what we're paying attention to. This is part of guarding our hearts: being careful what we allow into our hearts. Proverbs 4:23 says, *Above all else, guard your heart for it is the wellspring of life.*

In other words, did that nice, fun little movie you just watched reinforce godly principles of Kingdom living in the Spirit. Or did it reinforce worldly, anti-God, sinful, or even demonic mindsets?

There is much talk in our culture these days of vegging, and it has nothing to do with eating healthy. It is this idea of lying around virtually doing nothing. In reality, we're not doing nothing. Usually when we say that, we're talking about spending large chunks of time mindlessly on entertainment.

Binge watching T.V. and movies causes our minds to wander. The media does its thinking for us as we sit back and are not assertive with our thought life.

You may be tempted to think that what I'm saying is extreme and say, "Oh, it's not a problem; media and entertainment don't affect me that way." If that is the case, hallelujah! That's great. But let me ask you, when you go to quiet your mind and heart before the Lord to engage His presence, is what comes up on the screen of your mind what you saw on the T.V., computer, or movie screen the night before or earlier in the week?

This isn't meant to be strict and harsh. It is simply meant for us to think about what we think about, so we can discipline our thought life, in order to easily and effectively enter Papa's presence.

Some of the things which may pop up on the screen of your mind might not be sinful, wicked things, but simply are distractions. Lest you think I'm personally being too extreme, consider what Paul says about the enemies of the cross of Christ in Philippians 3:19b: *Their mind is on earthly things.*

You might be tempted to say, "Whoa, wait a minute here. We don't want to get too carried away and be too heavenly minded." But in the very next verse Paul says, *But our citizenship is in heaven.* He is making a clear contrast here by saying the enemies of the cross of Christ think about earthly things, but we on the other hand, as followers of Jesus... our citizenship is in heaven.

The holy atmosphere of heaven, with pure peace and perfect love, is the natural habitat for the born-again believer. This makes sense if we understand that we were born again from above (John 3:3), and that we are seated with Christ in heavenly places (Ephesians 2:6).

Most of us have heard the phrase that some people are so heavenly minded, they're no earthly good.

Frankly, I've never met anyone like that. Maybe Enoch was that way, and that's why God just took him home. I really don't know. That was long before I was born.

I think Jesus was the most heavenly minded person to ever walk the Earth, and He is after all our example. He was so heavenly minded, and He brought about the greatest good on Earth.

The point is that what we do with our lives, what we think about and focus on, affects our ability to concentrate on the Lord and enter His presence.

Have you ever watched a movie at night, then gone to bed and woke up the next morning, and realized that some of that movie crept into your dreams? This isn't necessarily good or bad. It depends on the movie. Have you ever had conversations with people before you went to bed and those same people or maybe the stories you talked about wound up in your dreams?

Why is that? It's because what we allow into our brains comes out in different ways at different times. So, what is the answer to this? Combining those two scriptures of Romans 12:2 and Philippians 3:19b, we see that we need to make a clean break with worldly patterns of thinking and have our minds renewed according to our citizenship in heaven.

Paul also says in Colossians 3:1-2, *Since, then, you have been raised with Christ, set your hearts on things above, where Christ is seated at the right hand of God. Set your minds on things above, not on Earthly things.*

We will conclude this chapter by recognizing that this is not a matter of legalism; it's about adding intentionality to our passion to be in Papa's presence. Obviously, we are to say *no* to all sinful forms of entertainment, but at the heart of this is simply learning how to overcome distractions in our minds.

As you learn to conquer the distractions in your mind more and more, you will be able to quiet your heart and mind before the Lord and more easily enter into and live in His presence.

Here are some verses that address our thinking. I want to encourage you to think about these verses that talk about our thinking.

Cast all your anxiety on Him because He cares for you. 1 Peter 4:7

You keep him in perfect peace whose mind is stayed on You, because he trusts in You. Isaiah 26:3 ESV

Finally, brothers, whatever is true, whatever is noble, whatever is right, whatever is pure, whatever is

lovely, whatever is admirable – if anything is excellent or praiseworthy – think about such things. Philippians 4:8

But the fruit of the Spirit... is self-control. Galatians 5:23

For as he thinketh in his heart, so is he. Proverbs 23:7a

Let the wicked forsake his way, and the unrighteous man his thoughts; let him return to the Lord, that He may have compassion on him, and to our God, for He will abundantly pardon. For My thoughts are not your thoughts, and neither are My ways your ways declares the Lord. For as the heavens are higher than the earth, so are My ways higher than your ways and My thoughts higher than your thoughts. Isaiah 55:7-9

Chapter 16

GOD IS ALREADY ATTRACTED TO YOU

In the church, when we speak of pursuing God, seeking His face, or drawing near to Him, one of the challenges we run into is our concept, or rather misconception of who God is. There are some who would teach that because we are now in the New Covenant under grace with the indwelling of the Holy Spirit, there is no need to pursue God as we already have Him.

While it is theologically true that we "have Him", that doesn't mean that all of us are experiencing all of God in every area of our lives. Any theological concept that is only understood in a vacuum, that is to say only in theory not in relationship, can easily lead us astray.

Let's apply this concept to marriage. Hallelujah, my girlfriend agreed to marry me. We had a covenant ceremony called a wedding, and now we're in a marriage relationship. Now I don't have to seek her, I don't have to pursue her or seek her face. Does this sound odd?

It does sound rather odd, because most of us never speak like this referring to our spouse. It is true that I don't have to seek my wife in the sense that I lost her. I didn't accidently leave her at the mall. It's not like she ran off with a cowboy from Wyoming, and I have to go track her down. At the same time, just because we're married does it mean it's okay for me to stop pursuing her heart? Does it mean it's okay for the romance to cease and for me to stop growing in my love, honor, and appreciation of her?

She would tell you, no, it's not okay! (By the way, if I ever did leave her at the mall or if she ran off to Wyoming, I would chase her down in either circumstance.)

For those who would say that in the New Covenant, we already have it all in the finished work of the cross, I get it. I appreciate that. What we're not talking about is seeking after God as someone who doesn't know Him and is seeking to find salvation. We have discovered what true salvation in Christ alone is: "by grace through faith."

Now having discovered true salvation in Christ, we are no longer seeking for salvation, rather we are seeking to know the God of our salvation even more. I no longer pursue my wife so she will marry me; we're already married. I do pursue to know her more and to love her better.

There has been much debate, especially in the last century, over how much of the Holy Spirit believers have. Many would say that we get all of the Holy Spirit there is to get at salvation. Theologically, I understand why they say this. Perhaps a better question for us to ask is not how much of the Holy Spirit do we have, but rather how much does the Holy Spirit have of us?

This is more of a question of sanctification. That being, have we allowed Him to conform us to the image of Jesus and make us holy in every area of our lives? Regardless of what our theological persuasion is, though we rejoice in being adopted as sons, maturity is a whole other matter. God was not satisfied to just save us from hell, He wants mature sons who look like Jesus and reflect His nature and His Kingdom to others on Earth.

When we speak of seeking God, sometimes people erroneously think we are trying to get God to pay attention to us or that we are trying to twist His arm to get Him to notice us. This misconception stems from our misunderstanding of God's disposition towards us.

What is very helpful to understand at the outset of pursuing a lifestyle of living in His presence, is that God already has a preexisting condition. What do I mean by that? What I mean is God is love. It's His nature. It's His character. It's the essence of who He is. He was that way long before you ever called out to Him. That's why I say He has a preexisting condition. It's not a sickness, but you could say that He is lovesick.

For many of us, loving people is something we have to strain and struggle to do. If you think that this does not describe you, consider this: the Bible says love *is* patient. In other words, anytime you've struggled with patience, you've struggled with love. Does that help put it in perspective?

To truly love someone perfectly and unconditionally is very difficult even for the very best of us. But God simply *is* love. It's not something He tries to do, nor is it something He tries to be. He simply *is* love.

Even when we read in Scripture about His wrath, judgment, and even hell itself, we must remember that everything He does is rooted in perfect love.

Paul says in Romans 5:6 NIV, *You see, at just the right time, when we were still powerless, Christ died for the ungodly.*

Then Paul says in Romans 5:10a NIV *while we were God's enemies, we were reconciled to Him through the death of His Son.*

What does this tell us? While we were still godless sinners, God the Father pursued *us* by sending

Jesus to die on the cross. While we are to pursue a lifestyle of intimacy with the Father, living in His presence, we need to understand first of all that He pursued us long before we ever thought of pursuing Him. This is called grace. This is called love. This is amazing!

In all my pursuit of a deeper intimacy with my heavenly Father, I can never allow myself to forget that He's the One who initiated all of this. He's the One who took the first step towards me. All I can do is surrender and reciprocate His love.

The issue of sin is a really big deal, but that's why He sent Jesus to deal with the sin that causes separation from God by shedding His blood at the cross. Herein is where the problem lies: many believers believe that God loves them because Jesus went to the cross. They don't realize that Jesus was sent to the cross because God the Father has *always* loved them.

Jesus' death on the cross to remove our sins was not the goal. It was a means to an end. The goal was to restore us back into right relationship and intimate fellowship with the Father.

I'm sure you know John 3:16 which says, *For God so loved the world that He gave His one and only Son.*

Did God see all the wickedness, evil and corruption in the world and in His holiness hate all the sin He saw? Yes. He hated sin then, before the cross and He hates sin now, after the cross. His holiness has not changed. But what is it that motivates Him? What is His preexisting condition that determines why He does what He does?

John 3:16 does not say for God so hated sinners that He gave His only begotten Son. It does not say that God is so just that He gave His only begotten Son. Is God just? Yes. Is He holy? Absolutely, yes, but we have it clearly spelled out in John 3:16. His motivating factor *is* Love.

In Genesis chapter 3 when man sinned, God obviously knew that Adam and Eve had sinned. Yet, He still pursued them, walking toward them in the cool of the day, calling out with the loving heart of a broken Father. What He didn't ask was, "What did you do?" referring to their sin, as horrible and tragic as that was. What He called out was, "Where are you?" His focus was their lack of proximity to Himself.

In spite of already knowing that they had sinned, He still chose to draw near. He not only drew near, but in verse 21 it speaks of God making clothes to cover them. This is a beautiful picture of the heart of our loving Father that pursues us even in our sin and is ready to clothe us and cover our shame when we honestly confess our sin and failure to Him.

The idea that we need to get from all of this is that God's heart has always been toward us with an everlasting love. On our worst day as rebellious, arrogant sinners who cared nothing of God or His ways, with all of our sin and folly in His plain view, He still chose to send Jesus to the cross and never once regretted it.

In spite of all this, we have a tendency at times to think things like, "I've been walking with the Lord a number of years now, and I've messed up recently. Maybe He doesn't love me anymore."

Ha! That's ridiculous. He loved you before you were ever born (Ephesians 1:3) and loved you when you were His enemy (Romans 5:10). Do you really think that now that you've surrendered to follow, love, and worship Him, your recent struggles could actually cause Him to stop loving you?

In Luke 15:11-31 Jesus talks about the prodigal son. At least that's how we've usually heard it referred to, but really, it's a story about an extravagantly loving father. As you read the story, keep in mind the heart of the father toward the son. It says that while the son was still a long way off, the father saw him. How was it that he saw him when he was still a far way off? I believe it was because every day the father was looking, longing, and waiting for his son to come home.

What is the father's response when the son arrives? He doesn't yell or scream at him. He doesn't berate of shame him. As a matter of fact, he runs toward his son.

While it is true that God really hates sin, He still loves you. On your worst day, in your worst condition, when you were still lost in your sin, Papa was looking and waiting for you to come home to Him.

Not only did the father embrace his son in his filthy condition, but in spite of his filth he also kissed him. In spite of how much God hates sin and what it does to us, He simply cannot and will not stop loving us because it's who He is.

The beautiful part of this is that while the father embraced and kissed his son in all of his stench and shame, he didn't leave him that way. He immediately called for the best robe to be put on him, a ring for his fingers, and sandals for his feet. He did all of this because he refused to leave his son in that shameful condition, just as God the Father clothes us with the righteousness of Christ and removes our sin and shame.

Remember as you embark upon a journey of living in Papa's presence, that the moment you take one step toward Him, He's already been running after you!

Chapter 17

ENDLESS SUPPLY

You are the God of endless supply,

You are my Father, El Shaddai,

Your river of blessing always flows

and never runs dry.

Years ago, when God began to transform my life and manifest His presence powerfully to me, I remember thinking at times, *God, this is great. I love how Your presence just keeps coming. It's so wonderful, but is it going to stop?*

I had experienced touches of His presence in the past, but after a short while His presence would dissipate. Not only had this been my continued experience, I knew it was also the experience of others.

At this point I had gone from experience to expectation. It was then that the Lord told me, "Christopher, I'm giving you an inexhaustible anointing."

In this He wasn't telling me that I was someone or something special. He was just reassuring me that what He had given me was given to me to keep forever. In light of this, I want us to look at a few passages about this subject in the book of John.

When you think of all the miracles that Jesus performed, his opening of blind eyes and deaf ears, the casting out of demons, and raising the dead, which miracle do you think of as revealing His glory? Perhaps all of them, but Scripture doesn't say that He revealed His glory by all of these miracles. Do you remember what Jesus' first miracle was?

For hundreds and hundreds of years the Jews were eagerly waiting for the arrival of the Messiah. They wondered when God would finally show up on the scene and rescue them. After four hundred years of no prophetic witness, finally John the Baptist arrived on the scene and prepared the way for Jesus the Messiah.

After all the years, decades, and centuries of eager anticipation, what would be His inaugural miracle? There were so many needs around Him. So many people had great need just like today. There were sick who needed to be healed, demonized people who needed to be delivered, and bound ones who needed to be freed. Yet, what was His first miracle? He turned water into wine.

What?! Wait a minute. That doesn't sound very Messiah-like, godly, or religious. Why would He do such a thing? I don't know all the reasons, but the time He actually did it, it must've been God's will. Let's take a look at the passage.

On the third day a wedding took place at Cana of Galilee. Jesus' mother was there, and Jesus and His disciples had also been invited to the wedding.

When the wine was gone Jesus' mother said to Him, "They have no more wine."

"Dear woman, why do you involve Me?" Jesus replied, "My time has not yet come."

His mother said to the servants, "Do whatever He tells you."

Nearby stood six stone water jars, the kind used by the Jews for ceremonial washing, each holding from twenty to thirty gallons.

Jesus said to the servants, "Fill the jars with water,"; so they filled them to the brim. Then He told them, "Now draw some out and take it to the master of the banquet."

They did so, and the master of the banquet tasted the water that had been turned into wine. He did not realize where it had come from, though the servants who had drawn the water knew.

Then he called the bridegroom aside and said, "Everyone brings out the choice wine first and then the cheaper wine after the guests have had too much to drink; but you have saved the best till now."

This, the first of His miraculous signs, Jesus performed in Cana of Galilee. He thus revealed His glory, and His disciples put their faith in Him. John 2:1-11 NIV

What's fascinating to me about this is that if you go on to read the rest of the chapter, the other story that happens right afterwards is that Jesus goes into the temple, kicks butt, rebukes everybody, pulls out a whip, and drives the money changers out of the temple.

I admit this is perplexing to my religious mindset. I would think it would be the other way around. I would think Jesus would go to a party where people are drinking wine and knock over the tables and rebuke them. That He would be invited to a celebration at the temple where He would help the celebration to continue.

But that's not what happened. Instead, He does a miracle to keep the party going at the wedding and goes to the temple where He interrupts and ruins their religious activities. Does this challenge your perspective? I know it does mine.

As we look at this passage, I want you to keep in

mind that one of the symbols for the Holy Spirit in Scripture is wine. Paul told the Ephesians in chapter 5 not to be drunk with wine, but to be filled with the Spirit. And on the day of Pentecost, when the disciples were filled with the Holy Spirit, they were accused of having drunk too much wine.

In John 2:5 Mary said to the servants, "*Do whatever He tells you.*" That's just good, solid advice. Do whatever Jesus tells you.

Verse 6 tells us how much water was turned into wine. Now we know that if Jesus had even turned one little drop of water into wine, it would still be a miracle. But look how much water there was: six stone water jars each holding from twenty to thirty gallons. If they all held thirty gallons, they would hold a grand total of one hundred eighty gallons!

Isn't that a little extravagant? Isn't that a bit much? The wedding obviously had been going on for a while since by that point they had run out of wine. Jesus doesn't just turn a drop of water into wine, or even a cup or a gallon. He turns up to one hundred eighty gallons of water into wine. Was that really necessary? Seriously, don't you think that's a little crazy. Who really needs a hundred eighty gallons of wine, especially after a party has been going on for a while?

I grew up believing that God is a practical God (and He is), wise (and He is), but even conservative. In this story, He's practical by helping out a friend who ran out of beverage at his wedding party. That's practical, but conservative? That's extravagant. That's crazy, over the top.

The point is God has more than enough of the presence and power of the Holy Spirit to go around. He knows no lack. He's the God of more than enough. He's the God of abundance. There's plenty of the wine of the Spirit to go around.

Now let's look at another example of this in John chapter 6. The context of this story is a huge crowd of people was coming to Jesus. To test Phillip, Jesus asked him where they could get enough food to feed everybody. So, one of the disciples pointed out a boy who had five loaves of bread and two small fish.

Jesus said, "Have the people sit down." There was plenty of grass in that place, and the men sat down, about five thousand of them. Jesus then took the loaves, gave thanks, and distributed to those who were seated as much as they wanted. He did the same with the fish. John 6:10-11 NIV

In verse 10 it says that there were about five thousand men. In that culture, in that day and time, when crowds were counted, as pointed out by the scripture, they only counted the men. This excluded the number of women and children who also made up the crowd. So, if there was just one woman and one child per man, you would have a crowd of fifteen thousand people.

It says in verse 11 that Jesus took the loaves and gave thanks. The first thing that stands out to me about that is that Jesus took what was given to Him and didn't complain about the lack. He was not overwhelmed by the small amount of bread in light of the huge crowd in front of him. He simply gave thanks. He didn't complain and curse His lack; He gave thanks for what He did have. Once He did that, God worked a miracle and turned it into more, way more.

This principle is called multiplication through appreciation. This principle can be applied to any area of your life. Specifically, in regard to God's presence, what you cannot allow yourself to do is complain about what you don't feel, especially if you see other people being blessed by God's presence.

You and I have never done a single thing to earn even a drop of God's presence. Remember, He doesn't owe us anything. So, if it doesn't seem as if we're experiencing His presence, we still get to live in gratitude.

If you only feel a drop of His presence, don't complain about the lack of a flood. Thank Him for that drop because you never earned it. It was all by His grace in the first place.

Instead of complaining, if I simply give thanks to God for His love and that His presence is with me regardless of what I feel, that is a right response. It's a faith response and is pleasing to God.

Let's say I only feel a tiny drop of His presence when I was wanting or expecting a lot more. I have found that if I will give Him thanks for the small amount of His presence that I'm feeling, most often through the principle of multiplication through appreciation, He will increase what I'm feeling.

For years, every time I read or heard this story I understood that this crowd of people ate the bread and fish that were multiplied. That's what really happened, and it is truly amazing. But what I didn't see until just recently is what is stated in verse 11. *Jesus then took the loaves, gave thanks, and distributed to those who were seated as much as they wanted. He did the same with the fish.*

As much as they wanted? *As much as they wanted?* Wow! People not only ate multiplied bread and fish, they ate as much as they wanted of it. There was no lack. It was like a never-ending buffet.

Little kids got as much as they wanted. Old ladies had their fill. Big, burly men had as much bread and as much fish as they desired. It didn't matter if you were in the back row and four thousand people had eaten before you, when the basket got to you, you were able to eat as much as you wanted. There was plenty to go around.

In this story we once again find the endless supply of God on display. *Everybody* got to eat *as much* as they wanted.

At this point you may be thinking, "What does gluttony at a divine buffet have to do with God and me today?" Notice that it's this very chapter in which Jesus repeatedly speaks of Himself as the Bread of Life come down from heaven. What He is making clear to us in John 6 is that there is no lack on His end toward us.

Jesus Christ Himself is the ultimate Bread from heaven which He invites us to come and feed of. He reiterates this concept of feeding of Him in verses 57-58.

Who was it that determined when the miracle of the multiplied food ran out? You might be tempted to say, "Well, God of course. He's sovereign, right?"

Yes, He's sovereign, but He has delegated authority and responsibility to us. The one who determined when the miracle of the multiplication of the food would stop was the final guy who got full and said he wasn't hungry anymore.

The point is this: though our miracle working God is sovereign, He responds to our hunger. If there is any lack of the presence and power of the Holy Spirit in our lives, if there is any lack of the nature and character of Christ being lived through us, if there is a lack of the Father's holy and loving presence in our lives the problem is not on His end. It's always on ours.

Remember, He always responds to humility (gratitude) and hunger. Your powerful and always loving God every day invites you to come on into Papa's presence. In Psalm 23 He says He prepares a banqueting table before you. You are invited every day to come to your Father's table and feast and taste and see that He is good.

Chapter 18

WHAT TO DO WHEN HE COMES

So far in this book we've been talking a lot about how to enter God's presence, the right that we have as New Covenant sons and daughters, and we've looked at phycological and theological barriers to overcome to enter His presence. But now we get to the question: what do you do when He comes?

How should we respond we when start to feel His tangible manifest presence touching us? It's possible to get so caught up in looking at the different dynamics of entering His presence that we're left dumbfounded as to what to do when He actually does show up.

My simple answer to this question would be that Paul says in Romans 8 that sons of God are led by the Spirit of God. So, as a New Covenant son or daughter, the Holy Spirit on the inside of you can show you how you need to respond to Him each time. I don't believe there is a standard one size fits all answer to this question. Not only is God very diverse in how He manifests Himself to us, He has also made us diverse in our personalities, backgrounds, and how we're wired.

We also have to consider the diversity of different

seasons that we're in, and what God is wanting to accomplish in us in those different seasons. Therefore, I don't believe one basic answer can cover every scenario. But I do believe there are some principles that we can look at to help us along in our journey of how to rightly respond to the presence of God when He comes.

The main principle, above and beyond anything else we will look at, is the principle of yielding. When His manifest presence comes, do everything within your power, your mind, your body, and your spirit to yield to the presence of God and let Him have His way.

Scripture tells us not to quench the Spirit of God. Perhaps most of us think of that verse only in the context of a corporate setting with other believers. We can tend to think of not allowing Holy Spirit freedom to do what He wants to do in the corporate setting with other believers. That concept is a very valid application of this verse, but I want us to first take a look at it on a personal level before we apply it corporately to the church.

The church is comprised of individual believers, therefore, if the Holy Spirit is quenched in a gathering of believers, it's because an individual, or individuals, stopped the flow and quenched what He wanted to do. Whatever does or doesn't happen in the corporate church gathering starts with us as individual believers.

I have heard of so many stories, the opposite of testimonies, of people sharing how they felt the presence of God begin to come upon them powerfully and how they began to resist what God was wanting to do. I wish I could say that all of these examples were just from other people, but the reality is I believe at times over the years, to varying degrees, I've done the same myself.

There are times when the presence and power of the Holy Spirit will come upon us, and it feels awkward and uncomfortable. If it happens in front of others, it can be potentially embarrassing. Growing up in the church, I often heard repeated this phrase that I now believe is a fallacy: *the Holy Spirit is a perfect Gentleman.*

While I can't claim to know exactly what people meant when they said that, I can certainly tell you this: if what people mean by that is that He will never embarrass you, that is far from accurate!

How many of you remember wrestling with your pride (really that's what we mean by embarrassment) when the Holy Spirit first told you to lift your hand in a church meeting for salvation or walk up to an altar at a church to admit that you needed to be saved? Do you remember what it felt like and how you battled thoughts of embarrassment when He told you to tell your parents that you'd become "born again" or the embarrassment you felt when the Holy Spirit told you to break up with your boyfriend or girlfriend because you were now going to follow Jesus? Or perhaps you recall that sense of embarrassment when He told you He wanted you to share the Gospel with someone at work or at school.

Don't tell me He will never do anything to make us uncomfortable or embarrassed. Actually, He is not very concerned about our comfort zones. More accurately, He wants us to move out of our comfort zones. That sense of embarrassment we feel at the thought of obeying Him is actually pride that He wants to crucify.

Am I saying that every crazy thing done in the name of the Holy Spirit in Pentecostal charismatic circles is truly from Him? No, of course not. Do I even think that some of the crazy things that happen in my meetings are necessary? No, I don't. But I am convinced of this: the Holy Spirit, while He is perfectly loving and gentle and kind, is God. He can do what He wants, how He wants, and He doesn't need to get my approval in order to do it. He is God and has every right to demand my allegiance and the surrender of my pride and my own understanding.

Often when the Holy Spirit is poured out, there are dramatic manifestations of His presence accompanied by dramatic physical reactions to the power of His presence. Do I believe that's always necessary? No. There have been countless men and women of God throughout the centuries who powerfully encountered God and lived Spirit-filled lives and didn't exhibit dramatic outward manifestations.

Is shaking, crying, laughing, groaning, jumping, screaming, or lying prostrate really necessary? No, unless God says it is. What I mean by that is, of course I could not point to a Scripture to say that any of that is necessary, because objectively we cannot find that in Scripture. But subjectively God might be requiring you to do something He doesn't require others to do. This is where He begins to deal with our hearts.

This is not a hard-and-fast rule, but generally I have found that if there's something in my heart resisting, saying God wouldn't really require me to do that, it usually means He's trying to get me to a greater level of surrender in my heart.

Most of us say we want all that God has for us. We

want to be filled with the Spirit and to live powerful, productive Christian lives... but then we add our stipulations. Underneath all of that we still have the small, fine print underneath written on our heart.

I've seen many people take this approach in meetings: *I'm hungry for God and I want Him to touch me, but I see those people up there falling over and looking weird. I want more of God, but I don't think I really need to do all that.*

I would agree, all of that is not necessary, but I think it's healthy to ask ourselves the question: *What **if** that was the way God wanted to fill me up and transform me?*

You might think *Well surely, He wouldn't want me to look like that.*

Ok, maybe you're right, but just what if that is the means that God almighty chose to use for you to encounter His presence? Simply ask yourself why you're so resistant to the idea of Him touching you that way.

Is it because there's a particular verse you can point to telling you that it's wrong? Is it because the Holy Spirit is making it clear to you that this is not for you? Or is it simply because it's outside of your comfort zone? Is it that you don't want to look like a fool and your desire to maintain your dignity is greater than your desperation for more of Him?

Again, many of us say we are very open to God and hungry for more of Him, but we have many stipulations and fine print.

It's kind of like a convenient store that has their big sign up front that says *Open 24/7*. Imagine it's 2 o'clock on a Saturday morning, and you're driving through a city you've never been through before. Everyone in your vehicle needs a bathroom break. You're so excited to see the sign. You pull up to the door and get out to use the restroom only to find in fine print... *Always open 24/7 except for Saturdays, Hanukah, Christmas, Easter, Flag Day, and the second Thursday of every month, my children's soccer games, and my grandmother's birthday... and oh yeah, don't forget, we're closed during Sunday night football as well.*

Suddenly that convenient store is not convenient for you the customer; it's only open at the convenience of the owner. This is often how we relate to the Holy Spirit. We need to be open to the Holy Spirit 24/7, allow Him to do whatever He wants, and obey His leading.

Earlier in this book when I referred to the spring of our visitation years ago, one of the things I learned early on was not only the art of waiting on the Lord, but the art of yielding to His presence when He would come. I use the word *art* very intentionally because I believe in a lot of ways it really is an artform.

There have been many people in the world of creative arts who have come up with a brilliant painting, a wonderful song, or box office hit but then never did it again. If they're remembered at all, they're only remembered as a one-hit wonder. Why is that?

I don't claim to know all the reasons. I'm sure there are many variables that go into it. Possibly one of the reasons is that the one-hit wonder was the result of a huge spark of creativity in the moment, but then they never learned the artform of abiding in creativity and flowing with the creative ideas as they would come so that they could create more artistic beauty.

Likewise, there are many Christians who have had a powerful encounter with God. It was truly from God and truly amazing, but it didn't truly change their lives because they didn't understand the ingredients that go into the art of yielding to His presence.

Unfortunately, in their ministry, or perhaps even more sadly in their walk with the Lord, they simply became a one-hit wonder. They have an amazing story to tell about a powerful encounter they had with the Lord's presence in years gone by, but not necessarily anything to show for it today.

I believe this is *not* God's heart or intention for us. He has so much more. Very early on during that spring when God was visiting me with His presence, I began to learn how to just be still before the Lord and not let my mind wander, but to focus on Him. During one of those times in His presence, I felt the anointing come very strongly upon me. It felt really wonderful. That was the moment when I thought to myself, *Wow, I feel such a strong anointing on me right now. Over the next few days when I teach or preach or lead worship, it's really going to be anointed. This is exciting!*

As I sat there happily basking in His presence, I suddenly heard the Lord interrupt my thought process with these words: *Do you really think that the whole reason why I show up and visit you with My love and My presence is just to make you more anointed for public ministry? Do you really believe that when you seek Me in the secret place the entire purpose of Me drawing near to you is just to make you "perform" better in public ministry?*

Ugh. I was cut to the heart. I realized in that

moment that while yes, of course He wants to anoint us to preach good news, His main objective as a loving Father is just to come be with us as His sons and daughters. He loves to pour through us, but only after He first pours into us.

There is not a battle in the Kingdom of God between public ministry and private intimacy with the Father. It's never a question of which one; it's always both, while recognizing the need to have them in the right order.

As our Heavenly Father, God wants to pass on the family business to us as His sons and daughters. That family business is called the Kingdom of God. But as a loving Father, His first priority is to be with us and for us to know His heart, to love Him, and to receive His love.

Only as we spend time with Him can we know His heart. As we know His heart, we know His values. Only as we know His values can we rightly express His Kingdom here on the earth.

Yes, God wants to use our lives to impact individuals, families, churches, cities, and nations, but we can't give what we don't have. So, before He comes to flow through us, He simply wants to come dwell and fellowship with us.

Years ago, God gave me a word for a man of God who has an amazing global ministry. The word was simply this: *The Father says, I will take you as far and wide in ministry as you are willing to go deep with Me in intimacy.*

That man of God has never forgotten that word and has often reminded me of it as the Lord has impressed on both of our hearts that beautiful invitation from the Father to live out the reality of that word.

God has no problem with promoting, blessing, and mightily using you as long as He knows He has *all* of you. He wants you to seek Him in the secret place, getting alone with Him where you pour out your heart in worship and He shares the secrets of His heart with you. From that place of His presence, you get to overflow to impact others.

The Psalmist says in Psalm 23 *My cup overflows.* He's not just barely getting by with a half-full or three-fourths filled cup. He's not even just full, which would be great for him. No, his cup is an overflowing cup so that anyone who gets around him starts to get blessed and experience the presence of God. That is a picture of the supernatural lifestyle of a New Covenant believer abiding in the Vine.

PRAYERS TO GET YOU STARTED

At this point, I want to share with you some simple prayers that you can get started with on your pathway into Papa's presence. I want to encourage you not to quickly read over the contents of these couple pages. These words are meant to be imbibed, to be read slowly and thoughtfully as a way to get you started.

Quietly read out loud these prayers of thanksgiving that declare who the Father is and who we are in Him. If there is a specific word that seems to grab your attention while praying it, pause right there and slowly say it again until the truth of that word sinks deep down into the center of your being.

God, thank you for being my wonderful Father and that you love me so much. Thank you that you not only love me, but you like me!

Thank you for the cross, Jesus, thank you for giving your life for me at the cross. Thank you that your blood cleanses me from ALL sin and makes me perfectly righteous.

Holy Spirit, I ask that you unveil to me the height and width and depth and length of Father God's extravagant love for me in Christ Jesus.

Abba, I thank you that there is now no condemnation for those who are in Christ Jesus and that's ME! You're not condemning me EVER! Jesus was completely condemned for me at the cross, so I can now be an accepted son like Him!
The law of the Spirit of life in Christ Jesus sets me FREE from the law of sin and death, YAY, I'm free!!!

Father, I thank you for putting me in Christ and Christ in me the hope of glory.

Thank you for choosing me before the creation of the world. You chose me before I could ever do anything wonderful or mess up or sin in anyway. Thank you that before I could ever be rejected, mistreated, abused, judged or misunderstood by my parents or authority figure or leader YOU, God Almighty chose ME!

You chose me because you always wanted me, I thank you that there has never been a single moment of my existence when I wasn't wanted.

Holy Spirit, thank you for living inside of me, thank you for giving me the privilege of being your temple. What an amazing Honor to host your presence on the inside of my being. I thank you precious Holy Spirit that whether I feel anything or not that I know you dwell inside me. Teach me to honor you well and not grieve you in any way. I love you, Holy Spirit, I want to be more sensitive to your desires and your voice. I love you so much and yield all that I am to you, come and fill me up again even now.

CONCLUSION

Thank you for going on this journey with me, pursuing the heart of the Father and seeking to abide in His presence. It's my hope and prayer that the Holy Spirit has been able to take the simple words from this little book to encourage you, awaken hunger, and arouse a deep spiritual longing within you to live in Papa's presence.

My desire is that as you finish this book, it will not be the ending but only the beginning of your journey deeper into the Father's heart and presence.

The short prayers you just read in the previous chapter are meant to get you going on the first steps of this path. Feel free to go back and pray them over and over again.

Also, feel free to not only pray them again but to add your own language to the prayers. Begin to expand the prayers by adding your own words and mixing your own prayers with them. The prayers that I wrote down are to only be a launching pad to launch you into your own passionate pursuit of His presence.

I would love to hear back from you as to how God has used this book to strengthen and encourage you on your journey. You can contact me by email at pastor.christopher@heartlandstaff.com

May God bless you on your journey!

RECOMMENDED READING

Secrets of the Secret Place by Bob Sorge

Experiencing the Depths of Jesus Christ by Madame Jeanne Guyon

The Inner Chamber and the Inner Life by Andrew Murray

Bone of His Bone by F.J. Huegel

11265128R10094

Made in the USA
Lexington, KY
09 October 2018